The Narrow Boat Book

The Narrow Boat Book

Tom Chaplin

Whittet Books

To my wife

First published 1978
Reprinted 1981
© 1978 by Tom Chaplin
Whittet Books Ltd, The Oil Mills, Weybridge, Surrey

British Library Cataloguing in Publication Data

Chaplin, Tom
  The narrow boat book.
  1. Canal-boats – History 2. Inland waterway vessels – England – History
  1. Title
  623.82.9 TC765

  ISBN 0-905483-04-9
  ISBN 0-905483-05-7 Pbk

Printed and bound in Great Britain by William Clowes (Beccles) Limited, Beccles and London

Contents

Acknowledgments

Countless people have assisted in the preparation of this book, and I should like to thank them all.

In particular, I am indebted to Reg Arnold, who took great pains over the photographic work, and Richard Hutchings, Curator of the Waterways Museum at Stoke Bruerne, who provided invaluable help.

I should like to thank my parents for their encouragement and help.

Finally, this book, which was written in spare time, would not have been possible without the help of my wife, who has spent innumerable hours behind a typewriter.

I should like to thank Bratton Publishing Ltd for permission to use much of the material from the article 'Pickford and the Canal Carrying Trade 1780-1850' by G.L. Turnbull (from Transport History, vol. 6, no. 3); also Messrs Pickford for their help in compiling chapter 4.

I should like to thank the following for permission to reproduce illustrations: I. Hough (Figs 169, 168, 130, 143, 163, 178, 192, 205, 206, 179); K.M. Simpkin (Figs 170, 157, 120, 185, 158); Waterways Museum (Figs 173, 180, 181, 29, 30, 40, 55, 57, 87, 114, 132, 140, 141, 144, 145, 142, 148, 150, 151, 152, 182, 176, 183, 187, 189, 190, 191, 194, 195, 196, 204, 200, 209, 208, 210, 214, 215, 207, 159, 4); K. Steele (Fig 174); P.H. Chaplin (Figs 171, 23, 28, 12, 14, 15, 39, 16, 17, 20, 63, 100, 105, 109, 110, 113, 133, 149, 153, 154, 156, 162, 161, 175, 217, 218, 223, 112, 22, 147, 19); Miss C. Bushell (Figs 41, 38, 49, 52, 53, 98, 186, 188, 211); P. Froud (Fig 11); Blue Line Cruisers (Fig 13); R.J. Hutchings (Figs 56, 137, 177, 193, 202, 201); British Waterways Board (Figs 117, 118); A. Lewery (Figs 93, 60, 61); Mr Chapman (Figs 105, 213); H. Fenimore (Fig. 116); *Wolverhampton Express and Star* (Figs 146, 223); Amos Burg (Fig 165); J. Gould (Fig 184); Cadbury Schweppes/Birmingham Library (Figs 197, 198, 199); David Viner Corinium Museum, Cirencester (Fig 131).

Preface

When holidaying on the canals today, it is difficult to imagine what busy and important trading thoroughfares the canals were in a more prosperous Britain. This book traces the two hundred years during which the narrow boat traversed these canals: the design and construction of the boats, the firms who built them, the people who used them, the traditions of painting and decorating, the cargoes carried and the way of life of the boat-people.

My aim is to record as much as possible at a time when living memory and history can still overlap. I hope that the book will answer many of the questions that canal enthusiasts have asked during the last couple of decades, as the character of the canals has changed from commerce to pleasure.

TOM CHAPLIN
July 1977

Fig. 1. Map showing the complete canal system available to narrow boats. Today a large number of these canals are disused.

Chapter One
The Canal System

Even before Roman times, rivers were an important method of commercial transport; the Romans carried out extensive engineering works on waterways, and, as well as aqueducts, even built canals. The first in England was Roman, the Fossdyke, which connected Lincoln to the River Trent. Most trade began on the tidal sections of rivers and then gradually penetrated inland, to encounter difficulties such as droughts, shallows and floods. By the end of the seventeenth century, due to the demand from industry, methods of water transport had become so advanced that the 'navigations' (rivers that had been artificially improved by engineering works) were highly sophisticated. But the building of a totally new waterway – a canal – was not undertaken until the middle of the eighteenth century, when the Duke of Bridgewater employed the engineer James Brindley to build the Bridgewater Canal, which was finished in 1761. After this, the construction of waterways multiplied, since by then England needed even more desperately a national network of transport; the industrial revolution was retarded partly because of this lack. Agricultural progress also demanded better transport for such materials as lime for land improvement.

Though the canals provided a very important method of cheap transport in the early

Fig. 2. A lock-keeper inserting paddles and rimers in a Thames flash lock.

Fig. 3. A boat going through a flash lock.

years of the industrial revolution, they failed to maintain their advantage in the face of competition from the railways. However, at the end of the eighteenth century, the canals still seemed to hold most promise for the future. They enabled heavy goods, such as the all-important fuel for the factories – coal – to be transported at a price of one penny per ton per mile, which was far cheaper than the price for road transport. Materials such as stone for road-building were carried, and for industries such as potteries, there were other obvious benefits over road transport, where breakages were frequent.

The early navigations had to overcome problems such as differences in water levels, and also lack of water during droughts. The solution they evolved was the 'flash' lock; as can be seen in the engraving (see Fig. 1), 'rimers and paddles' were inserted into the flow of water, to keep a sufficient depth in the waterway, acting as a kind of dam. This held back enough water to float the craft over shallows; when it arrived at the 'flash' lock, the paddles would be removed so that the water level would be roughly equalized, and the boat, if going downstream, would be floated through on the 'flush' or 'flash' of water. If going upstream, it would be winched up through the flood of water with some difficulty. The invention of the 'pound' lock (the lock as we now know it) was therefore a great advancement; the earliest built in this country was in 1567. Many of the early pound locks had sloping earth banks, but the early Thames locks had rectangular masonry walls, similar to those with which we are familiar. The Bridgewater Canal was built to carry the small

Fig. 4. A steamer with butty in tow progressing up the Buckby flight.

Mersey craft called 'flats', which were 72 feet long and 14 feet 6 inches wide, and the size of the locks on the canal at Runcorn was designed to accommodate them. The canal connected the coal mines of Worsley to Manchester and Runcorn; when more canals were built to link up with the Bridgewater – mainly to connect the Thames, Trent, Mersey and Severn – they encountered more problems. Tunnels had to be driven through the hills, and the expertise did not exist to build a tunnel wide enough to take the 14 feet 6 inch flats. It seems likely then that the 'narrow boats' used on such canals, which were the ancestors of our present narrow boats, were made exactly half the beam of a 'flat' so that goods could easily be transferred from one to the other, and also so that a pair of boats could fit into a lock side by side.

When the 'canal mania' was at its height, private companies sprouted up all over the country to build canals. The capital required was huge, and many companies collapsed before their projects were completed. Those that succeeded had to recoup their investment by charging extortionate tolls (or 'tonnages') to the boats that used the canals; ironically, these high rates contributed to the switch of trade to the railways. Until an Act of 1845, the canal companies were not allowed to act also as carriers, so they had to rely for revenue on the tolls. The carriers, at least in the early days, were independent and small, and they had a complicated task negotiating the many private stretches of canal with various sizes of lock, and different proprietors. Sometimes the carriers consisted merely of one family and **their** boat ('**Number Ones**', as they were called). Later the growth of trade led to large fleets being owned by carrying companies (some of whom were also canal companies) and manufacturers would have their own boats, which had the added bonus of acting as advertisements.

Goods most suitable for water transportation were heavy goods – raw materials such as coal; other goods, such as perishables, were also carried, but they went 'fly', the fastest method of canal travel, together with the passenger boats, to which all other boats had to give way.

The canal system grew until, at its zenith, in 1840, it covered 3,750 miles (see Figs

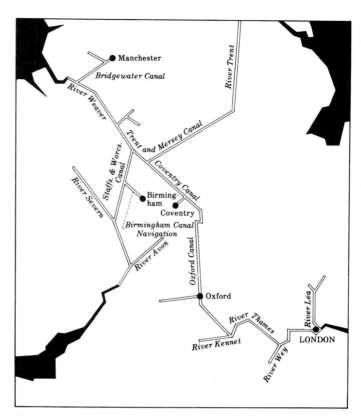

Fig. 5. Map showing the very first canals and river navigations used by narrow boats.

1 and 5). Unfortunately many canals were badly constructed – or even abandoned due to lack of funds – and the waterways with which they connected were unevenly maintained. The canal companies tended to protect their own local interests without regard to the national network of canals; had they pursued a policy of mutual improvement and universal standards, the competition the canals suffered from the railways might not have been so devastating. There was no uniformity in the sizes of locks or tunnels owned by different companies, which made transport through various canals by one carrier difficult. The Royal Commission on Canals and Inland Navigations recommended in 1909 that major canals should be enlarged to take 100-ton vessels as a standard, but this report was too late to save the waterways. When the canal companies operated their own carrying service, some held a monopoly over their own water, which again made long-distance haulage difficult. Though the steam locomotive inflicted the fatal blow to canal transport, the canal companies did not always act in their own best interests.

At the beginning, the railway threat applied

Fig. 6. The narrow boats Stanton *and* Belmont *approaching the coal wharf at Southall. The motor boat is on the right (with rounded stern), and the butty on the left. The cargo can be seen in the hold in front of the cabins.*

mainly to the 'fly' trade and the passenger trade; railways did not bother to attract heavy goods, and the canals continued to carry these until the tolls charged by the canals made the charges uncompetitive with the railways. But the canal companies were so terrified of the prospective opposition from railways that many of them sold out to railway companies. Eventually railway companies obtained control over a third of the total inland waterway mileage. Some canal companies grouped together and retaliated by also building railways: the Ellesmere, Montgomeryshire, Shrewsbury, Chester and Birmingham and Liverpool Junction Canal companies formed the Shropshire Union Railways and Canal Company, which built railways as well as canals. Obviously it was not in the interests of the railway companies to maintain – let alone improve – the canals, and so slowly they fell into desuetude. This was a deliberate policy by some companies since by law they were prevented from closing a canal while it carried trade. If, due to lack of maintenance, it was not navigable for five years, then the canal could be shut by Act of Parliament. Although the volume of trade on the canals during the nineteenth century did not fall markedly, there was such an increase in the total volume carried in the country, that in proportion it represented a large decrease.

Nowadays, canals are used as a method of transport for goods rarely – the only regular traffic being from Brentford to Boxmoor. Some narrow boats during the winter carry coal, and in the summer take boy scouts on camping trips. But the narrow boat as a pleasure boat is finding a new lease of life, and many of the old boats have been converted into holiday boats.

Chapter Two
Basic Design of Narrow Boats

A narrow boat can be distinguished from a barge, firstly by its size, which is narrower, and secondly, by the fact that its cargo is stowed in an open hold, whereas barges are usually 'flush-decked' (i.e. cargo is stowed in a covered hold or under hatches). The dimensions of a narrow boat, which give rise to the name, are approximately 70 feet in length and 7 feet in beam, carrying a maximum of 35 tons; the dimensions varied slightly according to the boatyard. The average draught of a narrow boat is 3 feet 6 inches when loaded, with 9 inches of hull above water.

Narrow boats were first built in the seventeen seventies, at which time they must have seemed very large, since even ocean-going ships were then not much larger; Captain Cook's *Endeavour*, in which he sailed to Australia, was only 100 feet long. Tradition has it that the first boats were designed by Thomas Monk (they used to be called 'Monkey Boats'). Whoever their actual designer, the early boats were probably built at a boatyard that built Mersey and Weaver 'flats', since the shape of a narrow boat is modelled on that of a 'flat'. Sadly, many of the boatbuilders who made the wooden hulls have now to limit themselves to repair works, and the construction of metal hulls is a new industry not confined to boatbuilders.

The early boats were horse-drawn, and worked singly, with the whole family living on board. The cabin was a small room at the stern, in which everyone lived, and the rest of the storage was used for cargo. When the steam engine came (and later the diesel), the motor was housed in another boat called the 'motor' and the old horse-drawn boat was towed behind and called the 'butty'. The motor took up, in the early Fellows Morton boats, about 10 tons of the precious storage space, a costly proportion. This was one disadvantage of the motor, and having two boats necessitated two people steering. Another disadvantage of steam power was that a trained engineman was needed on board. However,

there was a proportionate increase in cabin space, which was welcome; the cabin in the butty remained as the main living area, and the cabin in the motor was additional sleeping accommodation. The woman usually steered the butty, and so contrived to do her household chores at the same time.

Whilst the heavy goods were transported on either horse-drawn boats or in pairs of boats, operated by families living on the water, there were other types of trade carried on the canals. 'Fly' boats were the fast form of transport, which were used for perishable or urgent goods, and were operated by crews of single men, working twenty-four hours a day. The other kind of boats operating were the 'packet' or passenger boats, which were the Pullmans of the canals. They had two classes of comfort – both of which were luxurious – for the ninety-odd passengers. Packet boats were horse-drawn, towed by galloping horses, which were changed every four hours, maintaining a speed of ten miles per hour. The boats had sleek lines and a large sickle-shaped knife fixed on their bows, intended to slice through the tow-rope of any craft that dared get in their way. They operated to rigorous time-tables. One of the relics of this trade is the Paddington Packet Boat pub in Uxbridge. Here there was a regular passenger service to Paddington.

Many of the boats were owned by carrying companies, who employed the boatmen to work their craft, and supplied them with horses. The boatman would then be paid a wage for the journey. Other boatmen owned their boats and took freight on commission. In Birmingham and a few other cities, 'day' or 'joey' boats (that is, boats without any accommodation) were used for short-haul work. Journeys otherwise usually took a week or more.

The original horse-drawn, wooden boats laid down the principles of design which have been scarcely altered since then. As can be seen from the diagrams (see Fig. 7) the hold on the

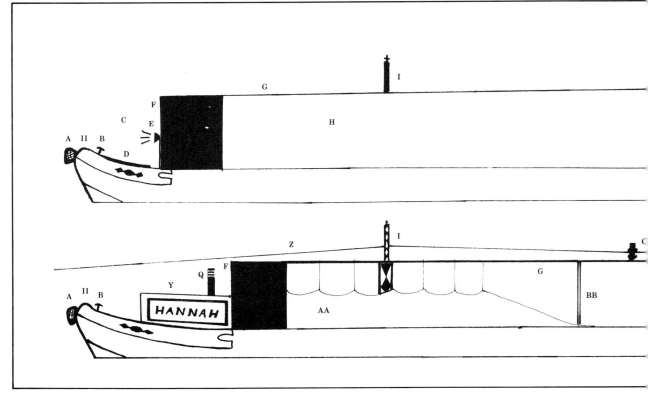

Fig. 7. The main parts of a narrow boat pair:

A, Bow fender	F, Cratch	K, Engine room	P, Water can
B, T-Stud	G, Top planks	L, Exhaust pipe	Q, Stove chimney
C, Foredeck	H, Cloths	M, Pigeon box	R, Removable tiller
D, Hatch cover	I, Mast	N, Living cabin	S, Tiller pin
E, Headlamp	J, Cabin block	O, Mop	T, Tiller

Fig. 8. The motor boat Roger showing the longer cabin, the extra engine funnel and the rounded stern. Note how there is a catwalk alongside the cabin.

Hannah commences about 7 feet from the stem, where the boat usually reaches its full beam at gunwale level. At the stem and stern of the boat is a wooden post (called either 'stem post' or 'stern post') to which the side planks are fitted. The post has a thick steel rim to give it protection. The area between the stem and hold is decked and forms a locker for ropes, fenders and other gear. At the fore end of the hold is a triangular board to which is affixed a wooden frame extending 3 foot aft and covered with black tarpaulin: this is called the 'cratch'. Recently variations have been rare: cratches without tarpaulin, and craft with a 'bulk', a framework with tarpaulin stretched over it, forming an elegant shape. In front of the cratch is the navigation lamp. In the forward section of the hold is the towing post, and, evenly spaced between this and the forward bulkhead of the cabin, are two more posts; these have flat tops and are termed 'stands'. 'Top planks' run from the cabin top to

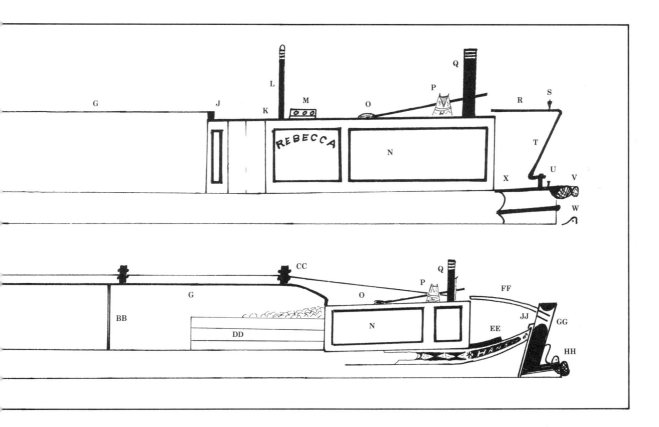

U, Towing pin	Z, Towing line	EE, Hatches	JJ, Stern post
V, Stern fender	AA, Side cloths	FF, Tiller or (H) elum	
W, Rudder	BB, Stands	GG, Ram's head	
X, Counter	CC, Running blocks	HH, Tipcat (fender)	
Y, Bow cabin	DD, Washboards	II, Stem post	

the fore end along these posts; the centre of the towing mast is telescopic and protrudes through a gap in the top plank. For cargoes needing protection, the hold is 'sheeted up' with sidecloths. These are fixed to the gunwale, and unrolled and tied to one another with cords which pass over the top plank. More tarpaulins are tied over the top of the top plank to provide further protection, and roped down securely. The final provision against the weather is a narrow strip of canvas which is laid along the top, under the ropes. The finishing touch is given by the set of white cotton ropes or belts which are run over the cratch end.

At the after end of the hold is the cabin; in a butty this is about 10 feet in length, with a height above gunnel level that varies according to the draught of the boat, in a butty this gives a head room of approximately five feet two inches. At the stern is a cockpit which gives access to the cabin and allows enough space to

Fig. 9. The butty Raymond *contains the main living accommodation. The cabin takes up the full width of the hull and, in common with most pairs, the butty is more elaborately painted. The large wooden tiller and rudder can be seen in the foreground.*

Fig. 10. A pair of narrow boats from the bows. The butty in this case has a bow cabin, although this was the exception rather than the rule.

wield the tiller. The tiller itself is massive and elegant, and it curves downwards towards the hatch of the cabin, from where the boatman usually steered.

The motor boat, here the *Rebecca*, follows the style of the original butty; the cabin is longer to accommodate the engine and fuel tanks, and it is higher since the engine weight keeps the stern down in the water when there is no cargo. Below water level the hull is a similar shape to the butty's, but above water it is rounded, and overhangs the propeller to act as an anti-cavitation plate. (This prevents air being sucked into the propeller, which impairs its efficiency.) The rudder head is of a 'Z' configuration, with a detachable brass tiller. The photographs on the previous page (Figs 8 and 9) show the differences between the butty and the motor. The early motors, propelled by steam, had even larger cabins and a large funnel.

Chapter Three
Types of Boat: Boatyards and Industrial Fleets

Throughout the history of the narrow boat, there have been hundreds of hull shapes, and variations in design. As it would not be possible to cover all types, we shall concentrate on the unique boats and those that were built in large numbers, always with particular reference to those used up to the end of trading, so that the description will help in identifying the different boats still operating.

Wooden Headers

These boats were natives of the Bridgewater Canal. Whereas usually a wooden narrow boat had a steel bollard (or 'T' stud), these boats had two wooden bollards, one on each side of the bow deck near the cratch. They were crudely built with such a blunt hull shape that they gave the impression of having been built without the need to steam the planks in order to bend them. They were of large proportions and were used on the Bridgewater Canal, where, since there were no locks, they were sometimes roughly replanked, which resulted in boats being over-width. On other boats this would cause extra wear or cause the boat to jam in locks. Their usual cargo was coal, of which a pair of boats could carry up to 64 tons. An occasional exception was loads of potatoes

Fig. 11. A pair of wooden headers tied up at Runcorn. The rather imposing shape of the butty can be seen moored on the outside of the unusual stern end of the motor.

Fig. 12. Nurser's dockyard at Braunston in 1959. The boats were built under the corrugated iron shed on the left, behind which are two dry docks. The boats were painted at the covered dock in the background of the photograph.

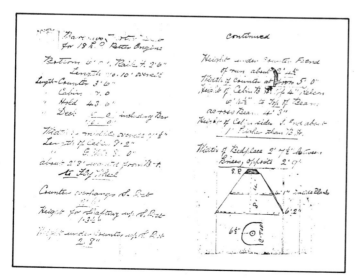

Fig. 13. Excerpts from Charles Nurser's note book.

carried from Acton Bridge on the Trent and Mersey to Manchester.

Because of their very high sides, the cabins were low. The motor boats were unlike any other type of motor, being basically the same as the butty with the same rudder and height of cabin, the main difference being the vertical sheathing (extra vertical planking nailed on top of the hull) round the stern. Like the butty, there was no rise to the stern. One of the last firms trading with these boats was John Horsefield, whose boats were docked at Simpson Davies boatyard, in an old basin round the back of Crosville's bus depot in Runcorn.

Nurser

This was the last boatyard to build wooden narrow boats; the boats they produced were very typical of the wooden boats built by the large number of small yards throughout the country. Both the boats and the paintings could be called truly traditional. The boatyard was founded in 1870 by Mr William Nurser at Braunston, and he later had two dockyards there. He was succeeded by his eldest son, William, who, due to illness, gave up the business in 1927. In 1928 the boatyard was re-formed as Nurser Bros by Charles and Frank Nurser, brothers of William Jnr, and a third partner, Thomas Hitchman. Frank Nurser was responsible for the painting and the office work; Charles Nurser, who incidentally left Braunston village school at the age of thirteen, was solely responsible for the building of the boats, while Thomas Hitchman was a blacksmith.

The business was finally sold in 1941 to Samuel Barlow Coal Company Limited, one condition of the sale being that Charles Nurser should give whatever assistance was necessary to Barlow's foreman whenever a new boat was built, while Frank stayed on as manager. In fact, the last boat to be launched there was the butty *Raymond* in 1958. Soon afterwards, the yard was sold to Blue Line Cruisers, which was the last firm regularly carrying coal in the south to 1970.

Instead of working from detailed plans, as did large yards, all necessary information at Nurser's was kept in note form in a paper-covered cash-book of some twenty pages, including necessary rough sketches.

The boats themselves had a 6 foot 10 inch rake to the stem, which gave it an elegantly long curve and a tall mast stand and cratch, which necessitated the aft stern plank curving down to a block resting on the cabin top. The cabin sides were devoid of panels and the name band tapered to the stern as the stern deck rose.

As they often carried a bulky type of coal, washboards, about 10 foot in length, were usually fitted forward of the cabin to allow a quantity of the cargo to be stacked well above gunwale level at the aft end of the hold.

These boats, being hand-built without drawings, differed significantly enough to allow individual boats to be distinguished. It has even been known for a boat to have one cabin side a different dimension from the other! They were built with fine detail; for example, the horizontal member of the rudder, instead of being parallel to the water, would rise with a slight taper, and their general shape made it

Fig. 14. The Nurser-built butty boat Grace *moored halfway up the Atherstone flight, having just loaded coal.*

possible to paint them more elaborately than other boats. Fig. 14 shows the craft to its best advantage.

Yarwoods

Yarwoods of Northwich, who began boatbuilding at the turn of the century, and stopped in the nineteen sixties, were builders of narrow boats (and larger craft), for the Weaver and Mersey. They built a wide range of steel and iron narrow boats. Probably their largest contracts were with Fellows Morton and Clayton and the Grand Union Canal Carrying Company, as will be seen in the next chapter. They also produced a large number of station boats and Cowburn and Cowper boats.

These boats all had a characteristic stem which continued in a tight curve at the top and protruded above the level of the bow deck. The station boats had fine lines with long flattish bow decks; they were built for the London Midland and Scottish railway to be used as day boats between canal-side factories and canal-railway interchange basins. At later times some of these boats had cabins fitted and, because of the very low freeboard, the cabin sides were exceptionally high. More recently some of these craft have given trouble, as during their early working life they were horse-drawn; the lazy steerer would let them bump along the canal banks so wearing away the iron hull under water.

Fig. 15. The ex-station boat Dabchick *enters Cropredy Lock on the Oxford Canal bound for an Oxford brewery.*

Fig. 16. A pair of tar boats descending the Napton flight single-handed on their way to Leamington gasworks. The decked-over hull can be clearly seen.

The last remaining station boats trading were the *Heron* and *Dabchick* in the south, and the *Crewe* and *Birdswood* in the north, while a lot are still used in maintenance work. Incidentally, the L.M.S. also had some similar boats constructed of wood.

We shall describe in the next chapter the boats Yarwoods built for carrying companies. They also would build 'one offs' such as *Trent Number Five* for the Staffordshire Chemical Company of Tunstall; this was very similar to the royalty class, but built as a tanker. Yarwoods also built the *Beatty* for Samuel Barlow, and the last two pairs of narrow boats built in England – *Lindsay* and *Jellicoe*, and *Mountbatten* and *Keppel*, for British Waterways.

J. and E. Morton

J. & E. Morton of Milnesbridge had a small fleet of 60-foot-long narrow boats which were used on the 'short' locks of the Aire and Calder as well as the Huddersfield narrow canal; these boats were 'tar' boats, i.e. they were used for carrying liquids. Some of this fleet were built by Stephson's of Hawkesbury Junction. The Huddersfield Canal Company also had short narrow boats to serve warehouses at Wakefield.

Several Manchester firms had a couple of special short boats in their fleets for their through traffic, the best known being Albert Woods of Castlefields, Manchester, who built two such boats at Sowerby Bridge.

British Waterways

During the nineteen fifties and sixties British Waterways cut up a multitude of their narrow boats, turning them into tugs, ice-breakers, pleasure boats and maintenance craft. While they had their oxy-acetylene torches at the ready they reduced some boats to 60 feet for maintenance purposes on the Aire and Calder.

Around this time British Waterways developed a new style of boat, in both the north-west and south-east. In the south they had the 'river class' (no connection with the Thos Clayton River Craft which were named after rivers); their most notable feature was the hold, which was covered with blue fibreglass hatch covers, hence giving rise to the nickname 'Blue Tops' or 'dustbin boats' (the lids came off!). The boats had vertical stems which met 'swim bows' (i.e. underwater, the bows were shaped as a punt's); the butties had fairly rounded sterns which resulted in the flow of water to the rudder being interrupted, making them very difficult to steer. There were two variations of the butty: one with a standard plywood cabin and a fairly big well; the other with an extended plywood cabin housing a chemical toilet, but with a very small stern deck. The motors were quite revolutionary as they were propelled by a 'harbourmaster' – a four-cylinder diesel outboard unit coupled with propeller steering which made them impractical for canals. The engine was poised at the very stern and could be easily removed; the cabin was portable and dropped into the hold. These boats were named after three-lettered rivers e.g. *Dee, Ure, Wey*.

In the north-west, the boats were of the 'admiral' class, the majority of which were built by Isaac Pimblott and Sons of Northwich. They were named alphabetically after admirals from *Anson* to *Mountbatten*. The hold was covered in tarpaulin, the masts and stands being replaced by steel hoops and the top and sidecloths being replaced by large

Fig. 17. The stern of the British Waterways river class butty Dee *in 1959 on her maiden trip. The rounded stern can be clearly seen.*

canvas sheets which were secured by wedges against the gunwale. This, of course, made sheeting-up a very quick and easy business. The hoops were low and hence there was a very low canvas cratch. The Pimblott butties were never successful and looked more like Simpson Davies' motors. The motors had steel cabins, like the butties, and were more successful. The counter was low and squarish, with two rubbing bands. The bow tended to plough through the water rather than cut through. Because of this, the 'Mark II' version, namely the *Grenville*, had a rake stem. The last two pairs of admiral boats were built by Yarwoods of Northwich. The bows had a turned-over look; the hold was the same as the other

Fig. 18. Left to right: the Mark II motor Grenville, *the Mark I* Effingham, *and the Yarwood butty,* Kepple.

13

Fig. 19. *The admiral class* Grenville *on her way to Birmingham travels along the Middlewich branch.*

Fig. 20. *A pair of admiral boats at Seddon's salt works. Note how the butty on the left has a catwalk.*

admiral boats. The long tillers of the admiral class motors made them light to steer. The butty's main characteristic was the catwalk alongside the cabin, like a motor. Various criticisms have been made about the all-steel cabins, which were lined with fibreboard. 'No good for the portable' or ''ot 'ouse in summer; ice box in winter', but others realized that at a time when most wooden cabins were rotten, they had a sound boat. This was borne out when a ship bumped along the *Mountbatten* in Runcorn docks and just grazed the paintwork on the cabin side. Had it been the *Lamprey*, moored on the inside, it could have badly damaged the wooden cabin.

The sheeting-up of an admiral class boat was reminiscent of the *Oxford and Portland Cement Company* craft, 'the blue and white boats' as they were called because their panels were painted white with ultra-marine framing and large blue lettering. The hold was covered by removable planks resting lengthways on curved frames. The whole was then covered over by canvas and held down with strips of wood wedged into small brackets on the gunwales. The fleet of six boats worked from the cement works at Kirtlington on the Southern Oxford until 1929, when the works were moved to Shipton. The fleet was usually maintained at Tooleys Boatyard at Banbury, and two of their boats, the *Banbury* and *Oxford*, were built there.

In various parts of the country, specialist boats were sometimes built. *Ingram Thompson and Sons Limited* of Lion Salt Works at Marston (which even in 1970 was still producing salt by the old tradition of boiling brine), had special wooden boats built with an extra plank depth as they were only used on three and a half miles of the Trent and Mersey Canal to Anderton; the canal here suffered from subsidence and the extra depth made it a viable proposition. The boats were either pulled by a small pony or shafted by hand. The cargo was discharged into coasters.

The same canal was used by boats from the potteries. The famous 'knobstick' boats built by the *Anderton Company* were barrel-sided and of fine lines. They were used for conveying finished pottery, often at high speed, to catch ships either at Runcorn or at Weston Point.

Like other boats in the area, they had low cabins to help with navigation through Harecastle tunnel. The cargoes were very light, the china having much packing, and so some of the boats had a draught of one plank less than average boats.

Because of the relatively short haul and the high wages (mainly due to bonuses) on these boats, many boatmen had houses in Middlewich.

In the Birmingham area, where there was so much short-haul work, 'day' or 'joey' boats were built, with no living accommodation, since the journeys they undertook were less than a day. These had very blunt lines, the rudder could be hung from either end and the cabin, if there was one, was only large enough for shelter from the rain and brewing a cup of tea. Often these boats were used for such mundane things as rubbish. A boat would be moored at the back of a factory, and, after a week or so, when it was overflowing with rubbish and smelly chemicals, it would be towed away by a horse and replaced by a fresh one. Instead of turning the boat round, the rudder was just hung on the other end of the boat. Because of the nature of some of the cargoes carried, it was sometimes considered more economical to build the boats of deal (a cheap soft wood), and to chuck the boat when it was rotten rather than to repair it. These boats were either pulled by horse, hand or by tug. Because of the long lock-free sections of the Birmingham Canal Navigations, sometimes a train of boats would be towed behind one tug, although on these long sections, 'Ampton boats were occasionally used.

'Ampton boats were similar to day boats but were wider and longer (maximum size 90 feet by 8 feet 6 inches) and had a capacity of 58 tons. They could only work the lock-free sections and were used mostly for carrying coal from the Cannock pits to Wolverhampton.

A few joey boats were built of iron but were more conventional. The rudder could only be hung at one end. They were called 'Pig Iron Boats' and traded from Hatherton Furnaces. Some of these were later used by Seddons, salt producers of Middlewich, for carrying ashes from their works to the flashes (lakes formed by subsidence after salt mining) where the

Fig. 21. A tug tows two joey boats laden with coal to Stewart and Lloyd's steel works at Coombes Wood, Birmingham Canal Navigations.

cargoes were dumped.

Day boats were also used in the potteries but never to a large extent, and were often old narrow boats, while in the Birmingham area they sometimes travelled a fair distance, loading coal on the Coventry Canal as well as venturing on to the Staffordshire and Worcestershire.

Dickinsons, the paper manufacturers, had several boats built by Walkers of Rickmansworth and Bushell Bros which looked like conventional butties but were in fact shorter and wider. These were used on the lower Grand Union mainly between factories, and their shorter length made them easy to turn.

In the First World War, along with barges and other craft, a few narrow boats were built

Fig. 22. Empty day boats without cabins returning up the Staffs and Worcs to the Cannock coalfield.

of concrete. As far as can be ascertained, they were moulded at Cubitts Yacht Basin, Chiswick. One of the the few remaining examples ended up as a floating balcony to a luxurious houseboat once moored at Tag's Island, near Hampton Court on the Thames, and was later moved to Teddington.

With the Grand Union as far as Braunston always having had 14 foot wide locks, *wide boats* became fairly common; the boats were, in fact, on narrow-boat lines and barrel-sided, the bottoms being about the same width as a

Fig. 23. The last remaining concrete narrow boat moored at Teddington.

narrow boat – as one boatman discovered when he tied up at Braunston stop (then 7 feet wide) one very blowy night to find when he woke up that the wind and the waves had propelled him to the wrong side! These boats were successful because of their small underwater cross-section. They were used mostly on the lower Grand Union particularly for carrying gravel. Many of the wide boats came to grief in the First World War during military operations; they were towed across the channel and used as transport on the Northern French canals.

In this chapter I have tried to give a good cross-section of the different types of narrow boat, but, without producing a dictionary, it is impossible to list all the types; unique boats were built, for example, the *Basingstoke*, which was built at Appledore in North Devon in the eighteen seventies for carrying bricks from the Nately Brick Works to Basingstoke and Ash. Canals such as the Wilts and Berks must also have produced their own craft; even Pontcysyllte produced the Shropshire Union boat *Symbol*. Quite a few yards built more than just narrow boats; Bushell Bros of Tring, apart from producing narrow boats such as Blue Line's *Roger*, built a number of maintenance craft, and Nurser produced various fishing punts for the gentry. In the next chapter we shall discuss the types of boat used by the different carrying companies.

Chapter Four
Canal Carrying Companies

As the progress of the construction of canals advanced, so did the trade of carrying. Before the Act of 1845, enabling canal companies to trade as carriers, only one canal company managed to evade the prohibition: the Trent and Mersey Company formed Hugh Henshall and Company (Canal Carriers) and by 1795 had sixty-five boats registered. By adding to the possibilities of revenue, carrying made the canals more profitable. However, before the canal companies came on to the scene, there were many other successful private carriers. One of the earliest was John Gilbert, who was the agent for the Duke of Bridgewater; he set up in partnership with a road carrier, and they traded under the name of 'Worthington and Gilbert'. Since the Manchester trade had to use both the Trent and Mersey and the Bridgewater Canals, competition between Worthington and Gilbert and the Trent and Mersey Company was fierce.

Pickfords

Pickfords is still a big name in transport, and it shows their versatility that once they were one of the largest canal carriers. Thomas Pickford, the founder, had been a road carrier, before the canals, and he immediately realized the potential of the 'fly' traffic on the canals. He took over part of Hugh Henshall's business, and concentrated on the London to Manchester run. He adopted the Shardlow transfer point; goods travelled from Shardlow to London by road, since the Thames was not navigable. Soon afterwards, Pickford changed it to Rugeley, as this route was more direct. In May 1788, Matthew Pickford, who was then running the company, negotiated special rates with the Coventry Canal to compensate for transshipment past the uncompleted lengths of their canal, and set up wharfs and warehouses at Polesworth and Braunston, whence goods were taken by road to London. He was never keen on using the Southern Oxford Canal or the Thames to London, as the river was in such a poor state, at least until 1793.

LOCK	FIRST LOCK BUILT
St. John's	1790
Buscot	1790
Grafton	1896
Radcot	1893
Rushey	1790
Shifford	1897
Northmoor	1896
Pinkhill	1791
Eynsham	1928
Kings	1927
Godstow	1790
Osney	1790
Iffley	c. 1630
Sandford	c. 1630
Abingdon	1790
Culham	1809
Clifton	1822
Day's	1789
Benson	1788
Cleeve	1787
Goring	1787
Whitchurch	1787
Mapledurham	1776
Caversham	1778
Sonning	1773
Shiplake	1773
Marsh	1773
Hambleden	1773
Hurley	1773
Temple	1773
Marlow	1773
Cookham	1830
Boulters	1772
Bray	1845
Boveney	1838
Romney	1797
Old Windsor	1822
Bell Weir	1817
Penton Hook	1815
Chertsey	1813
Shepperton	1813
Sunbury	
Molesey	1815
Teddington	1811

Fig. 24.

That year the Grand Junction Canal was launched to link the Oxford Canal at Braunston to the Thames. The accompanying list shows the dates of the first locks built on the Thames. As soon as the Grand Union Canal was opened to Blisworth (Blisworth tunnel being the last bit to be opened) Pickfords moved their warehouse to Blisworth. Pickford's first London headquarters was at Paddington (on the Grand Junction) but in 1820, with a grant from the Regent's Canal Company, they were persuaded to move to City Road Basin on the Regent's Canal. They prospered and expanded, with boats travelling to destinations all over the country.

Surprisingly their fleet in 1795 was only ten boats, by 1820 it was up to about eighty, and during the eighteen twenties they replaced ninety per cent of their boats with new ones at an average cost of £192 each. The cost of this replacement over a period of five years was approximately one third of their profit for that time. By 1840 they had reached a peak of approximately one hundred and twenty boats.

The following account from the *Penny Magazine* of August 14th, 1842, gives a very good insight into how the company operations in London were run:

'At the wharf of Messrs. Pickford and Co., in the City Road, can be witnessed, on a larger scale than at any other part of the kingdom, the general operations connected with canal traffic.

'This large establishment nearly surrounds the southern extremity of the City Road Basin. From the coach-road we can see little of the premises; but on passing to a street in the rear we come to a pair of large folding gates opening into an area or court, and we cannot remain here many minutes, especially in the morning or evening, without witnessing a scene of astonishing activity. From about five or six o'clock in the evening waggons are pouring in from various parts of town, laden with goods intended to be sent into the country per canal. In the morning, on the other hand, laden waggons are leaving the establishment, conveying to different parts of the metropolis goods which have arrived per canal during the night.

'On entering the open area we find the eastern side bounded by stabling, where a large number of horses are kept during the intervals of business. In the centre of the area is the general warehouse, an enormous roofed building with open sides; and on the left are ranges of offices and counting-houses.

'To one who is permitted to visit these premises there is perhaps nothing more astonishing than to see upwards of a hundred clerks engaged in managing the business of the establishment; exhibiting a system of classification and subdivision most complete. In order to show the necessity for such an amount of mental labour, we may mention that the firm have establishments in nearly every part of England, conducted by their own servants, for the general management of canal traffic. In a map engraved for the firm the names of ninety-seven towns are given where establishments wholly belonging to the firm are kept up for the management of canal traffic; besides another list relating wholly to railroad traffic. At all of these places the whole commercial machinery of a carrier's establishment is maintained; so that a cargo of goods dispatched from Messrs. Pickford's wharf in London is consigned to their own servants at the particular country station, and thence delivered to the proper parties.

'Hence arises a most extensive system of correspondence and supervision, in which all the branch establishments look up to the parent establishment in London. In one of the offices of the counting-house, for example, the wall is covered by folios or cases, each inscribed with the name of one particular district, and each devoted to the reception of letters, inquiries, and other communications from the managers of the branch establishment to which it relates. In another department of the counting-house, with its own particular corps of clerks, are managed all the transactions respecting the horses, provender, boats, and waggons. The number of these, all belonging to the firm, is enormous; and every direction concerning them, whether relating to purchase, repair, or general management – whether relating to the parent establishment, or a branch establishment two hundred miles distant – emanates from this office. In another department is managed all the business relating to charges and disbursements; the rate of charge to be made at the branch establishments, and the general transactions between the firm and their customers. In a fourth department are managed all the transactions between the firm and the canal owners throughout England. The firm have stations on probably thirty or forty different canals,

Fig. 25. The scene of all the activity, Pickford's basin in City Road.

the proprietors of which establish rates of tonnage and general regulations independent of each other; so that the accounts with the various canal companies become voluminous and intricate. A fifth department in the counting-houses relates to the cash transactions, wherein the branch stations are brought into communication with the parent establishment as regards actual receipts. A sixth is the stationery office, in which are kept all the supplies of paper, plain and printed, for all the establishments. The printed papers are very numerous, and as each kind has a particular number attached to it, the manager of a country station sends up to town for a supply of any variety which he may require.

'All the above offices, occupying an extensive range of rooms in the upper part of the counting-house, relate to the affairs as a whole, serving to bring all the links into one chain. Below these are the offices in which the business of the London establishment, considered as only one member of the series, is managed. All the goods received from London to be dispatched into the country, the parties from whom received, the waggons by which brought, the boats into which packed, the persons to whom consigned; all the goods received from the country, and the steps by which they gradually reach the consignee – are recorded, and the general arrangements managed, in these lower offices.

'Let us now suppose that a London merchant wishes to send a cargo of goods to Manchester per canal, and that it is through the machinery of Messrs. Pickford's establishment that the transaction is to be effected. There are, in addition to receiving-houses in different parts of town, two offices, one at the east, and the other at the west end of London, where merchandize is collected for canal transit. Another establishment on a very large scale, maintained by the same firm at Camden Town, we shall not here particularly allude to, as it relates wholly to railroad traffic. One of the two town-offices, the 'Castle', in Wood-street, presents an animated and bustling scene towards evening, when waggons, laden with packages during the day, are about to be dispatched to the City Road wharf. On arriving at the wharf, each waggon draws up by the side of an elevated platform, provided with conveniences for unlading waggons and loading boats. From the southern extremity of the basin a branch turns to the east, nearly separating the yard into two portions. The portion on the southern side of this branch is called the 'discharging warehouse', and that in the northern the 'shipping warehouse'. The waggons, coming in laden with goods, proceed to the shipping-warehouse, where they are unladen, and the goods placed temporarily in groups on the platform of the warehouse. Each group is to form the cargo for one boat, so that there are as many groups as there are to be cargoes. The boats are drawn up at the side of the 'shipping warehouse', and are there laden. We will suppose that one is to start for Manchester that evening: into this one, therefore, are consigned all the goods brought by the various waggons from the receiving offices destined for the Manchester district; each package being weighed, checked, and properly registered before being placed in the boat. We saw on a recent occasion a large and valuable cargo of indigo, consigned to a Manchester manufacturer from a London house, and dispatched by the sort of commercial machinery here described. In each boat are placed packages going to places as much as possible contiguous to each other, so that the cargo may not be unpacked until it has reached its destination.

'At the hour of six or seven in the evening the scene which we have just described is presented in its busiest phase. As a general rule, all merchandize received during the day is dispatched by boat the same night; and as the goods are not brought to the wharf until toward evening, all the operations of loading and unloading are then carried on with great celerity. Each waggon as it arrives, draws up by the side of the raised platform; the crane is set to work, the packages and boxes are taken out; the clerks and warehouse-keepers prepare the requisite entries and invoices; the goods are wheeled across the platform to the edge of the canal; and the boatmen assist in stowing them away in the boats. There may be half-a-dozen boats dispatched in the same evening, all to be filled subsequent to the arrival of the laden waggons at the wharf at five or six o'clock. It is from this circumstance that nearly all the fly-boats leave the wharf late in the evening – sometimes at midnight – after the busy operations of the day are completed. The "captain", or chief boatman, receives orders as to its destination and proceedings; and he consigns the goods to the managers of the establishments at the country towns, from whence the goods are forwarded to the consignees.

'Let us, as a further exemplification of the nature of canal traffic, suppose that a Manchester manufacturer forwards a cargo of cottons to London by canal through the same agency. They are placed in charge of Messrs. Pickford's agents at Manchester, by whom they are dispatched to London in a fly-boat; daily information being conveyed from the country agent to the town establishment of the nature and extent of the consignments. The boat arrives at the City Road Basin, generally in the evening or during the night; and it remains untouched till the business hours of the next morning. It is then drawn up to the side of the 'discharging warehouse', where a crane speedily removes the cargo. Each package, after being weighed, compared with the invoice, &c., is placed in one or other of several separate groups. These groups do not relate to the places whence the goods have been brought, or the barges by which brought, but to different districts in London, and to the waggon or waggons going to those districts. All the boats which may have arrived since the preceeding morning are thus unladen, the contents classified, and waggons drawn up for this purpose to the side of the "discharging warehouse" are laden, each one with the packages consigned to one particular district. The waggons are then dispatched, and the boats wait till a return cargo is ready.

'It may easily be imagined that as every package is registered in books and invoices, bills and other documents, with great strictness, the amount of business transacted during the morning and evening is very extensive; while the middle of the day is occupied by other transactions of a general character. Sometimes a package, or cargo of packages, is directed to be warehoused at the wharf till called for; and for the accommodation of these a large area of ground is appropriated. In walking through these warehouses, goods of a multifarious character may often be seen, according to the circumstances of trade at the moment; Cheshire cheeses, bales of cotton goods, spades, barrels of ale and cider – indeed, all kinds of commodities are occasionally required to be warehoused for short periods, each warehouse being devoted to a particular class of goods.

'As the waggons and horses for the land transit belong to the firm, so do the boats also. Each boat is managed by three or four men and boys, of whom one is the principal, and is called the "Captain" of the boat. Into his charge is placed the cargo; he receives a certain sum for navigating the boat a certain number of miles, and out of this sum he pays his assistants. The proprietors fit up the little cabin which serves for "parlour and kitchen and all"; but the men supply their own provisions. The open barges which are to be seen on the Regent's Canal do not belong to Messrs. Pickford, they are the property of the merchants who deal in coal, stone, slate, and other heavy materials, and who have wharfs on the banks of the canal and its basins. Most of the coal is brought from the colliers lying in the Thames, through the Limehouse basin into the canal; but some is brought down the canal from the Midland Counties; as is also a considerable quantity of stone, lime &c.'

Pickford's expansion followed the canal building programme; with the opening of the Ashby de la Zouch Canal, goods bound to Leicester from London went to the company's wharf at Hinkley and were then taken overland. This arrangement lasted until August 9th, 1814, when two of their boats were among the flotilla at the opening celebrations of the Grand Union Canal (the Foxton-Watford section of the Leicester cut), and were the first boats to arrive in Leicester after navigating this new cut. Pickfords ran a runabout cross-country service using narrow boats that travelled from Leicester to Birmingham via Warwick, Banbury and Oxford.

The Grand Junction Railway was opened in 1837 and the London and Birmingham in 1838. These two were effectively the main lines out of Euston and, from then on, Pickfords started turning their sights to the railways. By 1850 Pickfords had disposed of most of their canal premises, boats and horses.

Pickfords by no means carried on all canals. In fact, narrow boats traded during the early nineteenth century over a very extensive area. South of the Thames, the Wiltshire and Berkshire and North Wiltshire were narrow canals but, because of the large amount of through traffic, narrow boats used all the navigations available. Salt from the Worcester and Birmingham Canal travelled through the Thames and Severn, and raw materials for paper-making came from the Erewash to Thatcham on the Kennet and Avon. Boats on the Wiltshire and Berkshire were seen by Tom Brown

(schooldays).

'There was the canal, by the way, which supplied the countryside with coal up and down which continually went the long barges, with the big black men lounging by the side of the houses along the towing path, and the women in bright coloured handkerchiefs standing in the stern steering. Standing I say, but you could never see whether they were standing or sitting, all but their heads and shoulders being out of sight in the cosy little cabins which occupied some eight feet of the stern, and which Tom Brown pictured to himself as the most desirable of residences.'

During these early years there were many large firms of carriers whose names today are unknown: 'Kenworthy and Company', 'Robins & Co' and the 'Cavendish Bridge Boat Company', who in 1780 had twenty boats, and owned many of the warehouses at Shardlow.

In the last of the pre-railway years when the fly trade was at its peak, it was dominated by about a dozen firms.

The Act of 1845 started a period of turbulence for the carriers, since they now had to compete with the canal companies. The impact of the railways was hitting the canal trade, but the large flow of bulk materials along canal through routes took over a century to dwindle. Out of the Act of 1845 the Shropshire Union fleet was born and stayed in

Fig. 26. The bow of a laden Fellows Morton and Clayton Yarwood motor.

21

Fig. 27. A steamer and butty en route to Birmingham from Brentford.

being until 1921, when it consisted of two hundred and two horse-drawn narrow boats. In 1854 the first fleet of steam narrow boats began with the launching of the Grand Junction Canal Company's *Dart*. After a couple of decades of rapid changes, the canal trade sank back into tranquillity and decline until just after the First World War.

Fellows Morton and Clayton

The original firm was founded by James Fellows of West Bromwich in 1837; later, it moved to Tipton. When James died in 1861 the business was taken over by his son, Joshua. The Grand Junction Canal Company gave up its fleet in 1876, and this gave Joshua the opportunity to expand. Frederick Morton joined him, and the company became Fellows Morton and Company, which continued to grow, taking over many small carriers.

In 1889 came the merger with William Clayton of Saltley, which gave the company the name Fellows Morton and Clayton. William Clayton was founded in 1842 and ran both conventional narrow boats and tank narrow boats. Its great asset was the dockyard at Saltley. At the merger, Thomas Clayton, the owner, became a director of Fellows Morton and Clayton.

Fellows Morton and Clayton became one of the largest and best-known of the canal carriers, having a fleet of wooden, iron and steel boats, of which those with iron hulls and wooden bottoms were famous. Some were built in their own yard at Saltley, others were built by Yarwoods of Northwich; even in the latter case, the superstructure was still built by Fellows Morton and Clayton. Saltley boats tended to have finer lines, with a counter, the bottom of which was very high.

The last Northwich boats to be built, the motors *Mendip* and *Malvern*, had more pronounced Yarwood stems (see Chapter Three), much deeper counters, and longer engine bearers, and were the first to have all-welded fuel tanks. The cabin sides were perfectly rectangular and panelled and there was a slight rise to the stern deck which was almost square in appearance. The butties were best identified by the hull, which only rose at the stern aft of the cabin and rose very high; the cabin sides, like the motor, were rectangular and panelled. The boats, in general, had little freeboard when fully loaded and had high masts and cratches.

Fellows Morton built most of their own wooden boats, predominantly butties, at their yard at Uxbridge, the most notable being their girl class starting with *Ada* in 1922.

The appearances of both their motors and

Fig. 28. Fellows Morton and Clayton's yard at Uxbridge just after nationalization.

Fig. 29. The Queen, built of timber at Toll End, Tipton, in 1887, by Fellows Morton and Company. She was sold in 1920 to Harvey Taylor of Aylesbury, who later had her converted to diesel by Bushell Bros of Tring.

Fig. 30. *A collection of boats at Paddington. Here there are narrow boats, wide boats, such as James Nixon's boat, and wide boats designed to go on the tideway like the boat in the foreground from which the picture had been taken. Note how the painting and the hull shape is common.*

butties were very similar to the steel boats, the main difference to the exterior being an extra set of rubbing bands round the stern of the motor, dividing the counter into three, and, to the interior, the fine panelling.

Some motors were specially built for Fellows Morton, for example, those for carrying tubes from Stewart and Lloyds; to accommodate the long tubes they had a condensed engine room length. This was done by recessing the fuel tank round the flywheel. Throughout their lives the boats often changed: the original boats had recessed panels with fancy grooves actually carved into the wood, but after repair, they sometimes had plain edges or no panels at all. At other times, a new cabin was fitted which tapered to the stern, while cratch masts and stands were shortened so they did not have to be taken down to get through Harecastle tunnel empty, and engine rooms were sometimes lengthened to fit new engines.

Fellows Morton had other non-standard boats like the *Emscote* and *Bascote* built by

Nurser. When Fellows Morton took over the Midland and Coast Carrying Company, these boats were automatically brought into the fleet, one such boat being the *Star*. In the south, they built the **Mapledurwell** and *Greywell* with washboards (to give added protection round the bows) and windlasses (hand winches used in docks) as they were used on the Thames and Wey and the Basingstoke Canal.

The painting of Fellows Morton boats changed from black and white to red, green and yellow after the advent of diesel. They also painted extra white semi-circles from the edge on both sides of the hatch on the cabin.

Thos Clayton were based at Oldbury. Their boats, often referred to as 'gas' or 'tar' boats, carried a variety of bulk liquids and the holds were completely decked over. Many of them were built by Nurser and varied from the standard pattern in that they had recessed panels and an extra band round the counter.

24

They were decorated with a particular style of rose, nicknamed a 'cabbage rose'. This firm always had wooden boats except on one occasion which resulted in an accident. (One interesting boat was *Umea* which was built to carry newsprint to Nash Mills on the Grand Union. Unfortunately on her first trip, it was found that she was just too narrow to accommodate full-width rolls; she was subsequently sold to Thomas Clayton and converted to a tanker.)

The hold was divided into sections with paddles between them so that the boat could be trimmed and the liquid was restrained from moving about in the hold. One of the largest contracts which this firm had was the carrying of oil for Shell Mex and B.P. from Ellesmere Port to Birmingham. The boats were all named after rivers, e.g. *Ribble, Usk, Tay*.

The firm was formed when Fellows Morton amalgamated with William Clayton in 1889, the tank craft from both companies, which were mainly supplied from Claytons, were transferred to a new company, Thos. Clayton, Oldbury, Ltd., which remained in existence until 1966, when a new motorway was built through their dock at Oldbury.

The Grand Union Canal Carrying Co.

The company formed in 1934, was based in London. This large fleet was built during the nineteen thirties and therefore these were by far the most common boats seen recently in the south. They basically fall into three categories:

1. Large and small steel motors and butties from Harland and Wolfe's yard at Woolwich, which are commonly referred to as 'large or small Woolwich'.

2. Large and small steel motors from Yarwoods of Northwich, known as 'large and small Northwich' boats.

3. Large and small wooden butties and motors built by Walkers of Rickmansworth, known as 'large and small Rickie'.

The Grand Union Canal Carrying Co. was formed out of Associated Canal Carriers of Northampton and London, whose first pair were the *George* and *Mary*, a large pair of boats built by a steel barrel works at Uxbridge.

This pair was followed by the 'royalty class', probably the best-known boat being the *Victoria*, renamed *Linda*, now owned by the **Birmingham and Midland Canal Carrying**

Fig. 31. The motor on the right is the royalty class Victoria, renamed Linda, while on the left is the F.M.C. Cypress. Both carry the same tonnage and so the proportions can easily be recognized.

Company. This class were of extremely large proportions.

1. Woolwich boats

The small Woolwich were of composite construction and bore names of stars and planets, which explains their title of 'star class'. Large Woolwich boats were generally of all-steel construction with rounded chine (where the side meets the bottom). They were named after towns and so are known as 'town class' boats. For easy recognition, all boats from **Aber** to **Hawkesbury**, with the exception of *Halsall*, are large Woolwich, and those from *Halsall* to *Yeoford*, with the exception of *Hawkesbury*, are large Northwich.

Fig. 32. A pair of large Woolwich boats showing the shape of the stern.

25

Fig. 33. *A small Woolwich butty. The non-rectangular shape of the cabin side and the shape of the stern can be seen.*

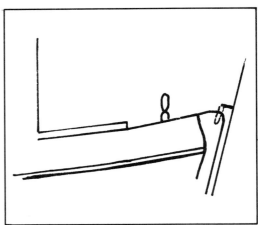

Fig. 35. *A sketch of how the stern plates meet the stem of a Woolwich butty.*

2. Northwich, large and small

These hulls had more shape than the bow and a typical Yarwood stem. The big were all-steel, with rounded chines, the small were of composite construction and had less freeboard.

3. Rickie Boats

These were built by Walker Bros of Rickmansworth; butties were large and small and motors small. All were constructed of wood. The butty sterns had a very plain shape; the large butties tended to look tubby. The easiest identification of a Walker boat is the way the stem meets the planks as shown in the illustration (see Fig. 38). The motors have recessed panels on the sides of the cabins and a fairly pointed stern deck. They are well-known for

Fig. 34. *A pair of small Woolwich boats* Comet *and* Betelgeuse *head south with a full load of coal.*

their handling qualities. Walkers built their last two boats, the butties *Aberystwyth* and *Bangor*, for British Waterways North-West division in 1953.

This now covers the basis of the Grand Union Canal Carrying Co. fleet, although several other boatyards were involved in building boats, such as Woods of Brentford, Pollock of Faversham. For easy distinction between large and small in any class, large boats were named after towns and small after stars and planets. The painting of Grand Union Carrying Co. was originally two shades of green and maroon; after the Coronation in 1937 it became deep red, white and blue.

Shropshire Union

Until 1921 a monopoly existed on the Shropshire Union Canal and only boats belonging to Shropshire Union Railway and Canal Co. were allowed to trade on the company's canals. This was a great advantage since the company's boats could trade into other railway companies' territories, and proved an asset even to the railway section of the company. The canal carrying by then acted as an extension of the railway, so the craft were fly boats and they were all horse-drawn. Since the fleet was disbanded in 1921, very few boats have survived into the 'seventies. The craft had finer lines than any mentioned so far: the bottom, taken on plan, would only reach full beam in one place, and the boats had long sleek foredecks with a large rake to the stem. The top plank sloped inwards, and there was little freeboard, with a maximum load of only 18 tons. One feature they had in common with other boats in the north-west was the name being carved at the stern. The boats were built

Fig. 36. The large Woolwich Dipper and Bedworth *with the same tonnage of coal; note how much higher they are out of the water and the extra rubbing band.*

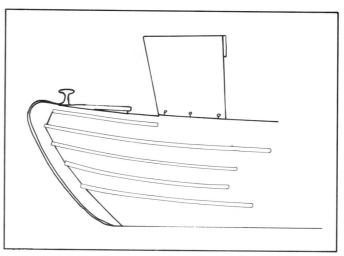

Fig. 38. An elevation of the bows of a Rickie boat.

Fig. 37. The tug Stentor *being built at Walker's yard. The stem, rudder and tiller of this boat were used for the new* Stentor *once owned by the author.*

Fig. 39. The late Tom Rolt's narrow boat Cressy *built for the Shropshire Union Canal Company at Pontcysyllte and converted at John Beech's boatyard on the Montgomery Canal at Frankton. This yard served several carrying companies including S. Owen and Son of Pant, Llanymynech.*

as far apart as Chester and Pontcysyllte and on the Staffordshire and Worcestershire Canal. After the disbandment of the fleet, they went to various owners; some, like the *Sir John Jellicoe,* went to A. & A. Peate of Maesbury Mill, Oswestry, while others, like the *Wisper,* which was built *circa* 1912 of green timber (about four and a half months from tree to finished boat) was bought by Fellows Morton, who in turn, sold her to the Erewash Canal Co.

It is interesting to recall the little traffic which remained until 1921 at the far end of the Llangollen Canal: cattle food was taken to Llangollen Wharf, and produce was supplied to local farms and shops from the large number of little wharfs; boats might just stop at a bridge hole to deliver a few dozen eggs to the local shop. The Shropshire Union offices were just past the junction bridge at Trevor

Fig. 40. The packet boat Duchess Countess. *She is seen in the photograph as a permanent home on the banks of the Welsh canal shortly before she was scrapped. By all accounts she had been altered very little from the days when she was towed at galloping pace down the canals. The rounded hull and sleek bows can just be discerned.*

(towards Llangollen) and here drums of oil and cattle food were unloaded. Stone was loaded at Trevor and was delivered to canalside wharves for roadmaking, along with porcelain pipes from Pontcysyllte.

A. & A. Peate's were the last boats to trade; they went as far as Frankton Junction and then down the Montgomery. They ceased trading in 1934; by 1936 a burst bank had cut the main part of the Montgomery from the Llangollen and only George Beck was left trading in the lower part until 1938.

The Shropshire Union Company had specially narrow narrow boats built called 'Trench boats' because they were designed to travel through the narrow tub-boat canal locks to the foot of the Trench inclined plane, on the Shrewsbury Canal Section. Trench boats were seventy feet long and six feet two inches wide; carrying seventeen and a half tons they drew two feet eight and a half inches. One advantage of these boats was the ease of locking uphill. The person leading the horse would partly shut the bottom lock gate on his side. The boatman would steer the boat into the other side of the lock and, as the paddles were drawn, that gate would shut automatically. The boats had very small cabins and there was barely head room to sit on the side bench.

One of the last Trench boats trading was the *Colonel*, which is now sunk near Anderton. Boats carrying cheese (Nantwich basin had large warehouses) in summer would have white top cloths to help reflect the sun.

The Shropshire Union painted a riot of lozenges on their boats.

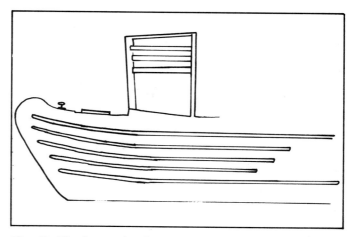

Fig. 41. The bows of a Cowburn and Cowper motor boat.

Cowburn and Cowper

This was a carrying company based in Manchester which began trading at the beginning of the twentieth century and still continues as a road-haulage contractor to the present day. Their motors, which were built by Yarwoods, were easily identified by their counters, which tapered to a point. This was advantageous when the motor was rammed by the butty, since, unlike some steel boats which became badly dented, here the bow of the butty was merely deflected. The bow shape was similar to that of Fellows Morton and Clayton. These boats were used for carrying chemicals, either in carboys or in tanks. In the latter case the boats were always sheeted up in the traditional way and in the bows, on the port side, there was a special release valve to flood the boat in case of fire or explosion. Built of steel, the boats had rounded chines and were used mainly on the Manchester to Coventry run and hence painted at Polesworth. They bore names of birds beginning with 'S', e.g. *Swan, Snipe, Seagull*, etc.

Chapter Five
Boatbuilding

Boats were either built in large, efficient yards or in small country premises run by just a few men who built mainly wooden craft. Orders being spasmodic, the smaller yards tended to diversify: they might be general tarpauliners, coal merchants, would paint vehicles (horse drawn), repair lorries and later, of course, pleasure boats. The basic rules of a boatyard were: 1. Never throw anything away. 2. No capital expenditure. 3. You have got to like

Fig. 42. Bushell's boatyard at Tring, Wendover branch, Grand Union Canal. Their wide range of activities can be seen. The signboard proclaims, 'Boatbuilders, carpenters and decorators', while the photograph gives evidence of the sale of coal and the construction and maintenance of pleasure boats, maintenance flats, wide boats and narrow boats. The Bushell yard was originally owned by Fred Mead, who had a fleet of boats taking hay and straw to London, bringing back manure. Old man Bushell ran the yard and built the Mead fleet; Mead sold his business and two of Bushell's sons, Joseph and Charles, took it over and ran it till 1948.

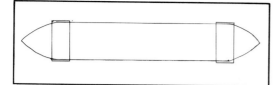

Fig. 43. The bottom planks were laid over-width as shown and trimmed up afterwards.

your customer before you will work for him.

In such a boatyard, time is immaterial and workmanship is first-class. Conditions were far from sophisticated, and it still baffles me how boats were painted in damp dry-docks with leaking tin roofs. Yet the paint stuck to the cabin sides like a limpet.

I shall now describe briefly the stages of construction of a wooden butty boat: the boat was built on a working platform about 1 foot 6 inches from the ground, and on to this the flat bottom was laid; the framework was marked and numbered into 'stations' from 1-13. These were used as references for the hull shape. If the builder were building a non-standard boat he would make up a mock side with thin lath (very thin wood), and then, using the station references, cut out a template to be transferred from the mock-up to the construction. On standard boats notes were sometimes kept of the dimensions at each station. The 3-inch elm bottom was laid across the boat with $\frac{1}{4}$ inch gap for caulking and laid wider than the boat. A few of the planks were slightly wedge-shaped so that they could be used for tightening up. The next job was to form the stem and stern post. This often necessitated an inspection of the local woods and forests, to find the right tree with a suitably shaped tree-trunk to form a curve without cutting across the grain. On these occasions the tree would be purchased from the landowner and the boatyard staff would help fell and remove it.

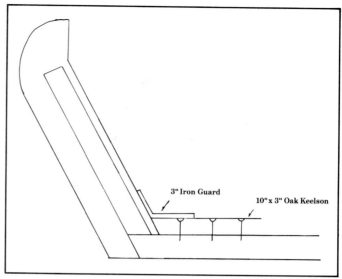

Fig. 45. Shows the fixing of the stem post to the rest of the boat.

Back at the yard, the posts were shaped up with an adze and a groove would be cut on each side to take the planks. These grooves were called the 'huddings'. The posts were fixed as shown in the accompanying sketch (see Fig. 45).

Before planking commenced a centre line was put down, and the bottom trimmed to the approximate shape with a template and an English oak keelson (a keel fixed to the inside of the hull) laid from post to post in 6 foot lengths scarfed (joined) together. This was fixed to the bottom with $\frac{1}{2}$-inch spikes and 5-inch long galvanized nails, riveted over, as the accompanying sketch (see Fig. 46).

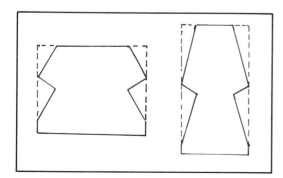

Fig. 44. Shows how the stem and stern posts were cut from solid timbers to receive the planks.

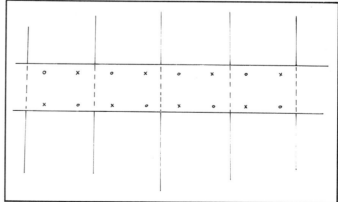

Fig. 46. The fixing of the keelson to the bottom planks; 'O' represents rivet up from the bottom and 'X' a 5-inch galvanized spike into the bottom.

Fig. 47. A very old picture showing the enormous clamp used just below the stem post and the shape of timber that can be derived with an adze.

Then it was time to start the planking. The planks had to be steamed to make them pliable enough to conform to the hull shape; nobody was keen to take the end of the plank which went into the huddings as it was the hottest, and could very quickly blister your hands. The planks were held in the huddings by an enormous clamp weighing over a hundredweight, which can be seen in the accompanying photograph (see Fig. 47).

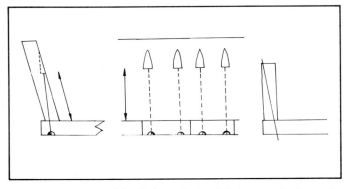

Fig. 48. The method of fixing a plank to the bottom.

The bottom planks were made fast to where the plank is upright, i.e. number 6 station (see Fig 48); from there, 11-inch spikes were used. Nurser Brothers of Braunston would have re-levelled the boat to a more convenient working height at this stage, but at Tring the craft stayed on the same framework.

The next job was to fit the 'knees' (which acted like 'ribs', to form the shape of the boat) which were 6-inch by 3-inch oak for bulkheads; 5¼-inch by 3-inch for intermediates. These were fastened with 8-inch nails riveted over. Dummy frames were fixed in the cabin space at two iron knees' space from the bulkhead. These dummy frames were used as fairing up frames. The boat was then ready to receive the rest of its planks. The bow and stern planks needed spiling (prounced 'spoiling'), that is, they had to be tapered such that when they were fitted to the boat they rose as they got to the stem or stern post. The difficult job in spiling was making the planks curve the correct way, for example a steamed plank when held up against the boat would sometimes naturally want to curve upwards in the middle rather than following the line of the lower plank.

Fig. 49. Boats in the covered dock. On the left can be seen the general working height and the supports to hold the stem needed in the early stages of construction.

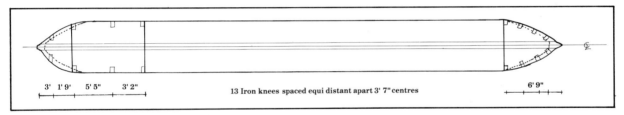

3' 1' 9' 5' 5" 3' 2"   13 Iron knees spaced equi distant apart 3' 7" centres   6' 9"

Fig. 50. The spacing of frames of the butty boat.

Each plank was shaped so that it could be removed at a later date without disturbing the other planks and each wooden frame was faired flat with an adze so that each plank butted up to it for its whole depth. When planking had finished, the next laborious job was to ensure that there was a constant thickness of caulking between planks and this was done by inserting a saw in the big gaps and cutting along the length of the plank to make an even width.

Having planked the boat, the inside of the hold was sheathed with soft or hard wood, and the gap between the two layers was filled with chalico (a mixture of tar, cow-hair and horse-dung heated) and paper in the fore and aft ends and tar and paper amidships.

One of the great skills was in the finishing off with the adze, which was like turning a 50p piece into a circle. At the end the sides would

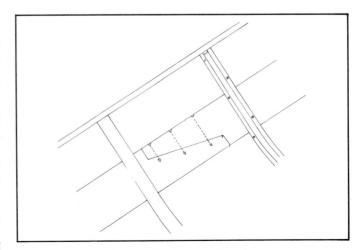

Fig. 51. The scarfing of planks and their fixing to knees.

Fig. 52. The gentleman in the foreground is holding an adze over his knee.

be as smooth as if they had been planed. The boat then was basically complete, although the making of the tiller and rudder called for yet more craftmanship. For the finish of the cabin yet another skill was needed to panel the small areas and trim the bulkheads to the traditional fancy shapes and add intricate grooving. The blacksmith's art was called for to sheath the bow to protect it from ice and fit a beautiful thick iron strip down the stem (also for protection). To protect bows and sterns of motors, a string of longitudinal steel ovals acted as rubbing bands.

Boats of composite construction had wooden bottoms and when they were built the hulls were riveted. The bottoms received most wear, and replacing a wooden bottom was easier than fitting a riveted iron or steel bottom. Non-composite boats usually had a rounded chine which helped them to navigate shallow canals better. Despite the belief that steel boats lasted for ever, many ended up with sides 'as thin as fag paper'. Certainly the quality of some of the iron boats was far superior to the steel: boats like the *Pearl*, which was once the steamer *Baron* and is now a converted houseboat, fully canalworthy. Another example was the *Lynx*, one of Fellows Morton and Clayton's first iron diesel boats, which when carrying salt in polythene bags suffered no side effects while the sides of the steel *Mountbatten* flaked when carrying a similar load. Repairs in some cases were carried out in dry-docks, and many boatyards had no provision for slipping boats.

When boats were painted, non-gloss paints were used – the old-fashioned type of pure colour in an oil base, the gloss being given by the varnish over the top. This gave a pleasant

Fig. 53. John Dickenson's Progress *under construction. The solid lump of wood which forms the stern counter can just be seen on the right.*

texture and the paint lasted longer than modern gloss paints. The paint rarely peeled, but over time it wore away. A boat needing a repaint would only look faded and bare wood would show where the boatman usually put his hand or where ropes usually chafed. Many of the last professional painters had started work at boatyards in the late nineteenth century and their memories indicate that, even then, the traditional painting had remained unchanged for generations. A skilled painter would complete a castle in less than an hour and could earn a comfortable supplement to his living by painting an extra castle or a

Fig. 54. *The completed* Progress *afloat.*

Fig. 55. Frank Jones puts the finishing touches to the Colin *at Faulkners of Leighton Buzzard. He is painting from a small punt afloat. The excellent quality of the graining and the very clear roses can be seen on the left.*

Fig. 56. The gauging lock at Brentford where unfortunately the weights shifted and the boat heeled over and sank.

bunch of roses for a Number One, charging him 5 or 6 shillings for less than an hour's work. Mr Fenimore of Bushell's would completely repaint a pair of 'Ovaltine' boats in two weeks; the work included painting 23 castles and 16 bunches of roses. I shall describe the painting – inside and out – of narrow boats in more detail in the next chapter.

Once the boat was afloat, the very important job of gauging was carried out. Boats were charged tolls on the tonnage they carried and the tonnage was calculated from the amount of water they drew, which could in reverse be worked out as the number of dry inches outside the boat, i.e. the distance from the gunwale to the water. The boat was

gauged after it had 'taken up' (that is, the planks had absorbed water) by placing weights inside the hold and taking a mean reading for four points on the side. This would be recorded and sent to each relevant canal company; when the boat entered the canal it could then be charged a toll without further measurement. In the case of the Birmingham Canal Navigations the boats had a small cast-iron plate bearing the registration number attached in a conspicuous position. On the Grand Union, every toll office had shelves of leather-bound folders, each containing the tonnages carried against dry inches for every boat registered and any amendments to the boat that might affect its weight. Some companies had the canal company's number on the side. Fellows Morton and Clayton had three numbers on the side – one being their own, the other two being the numbers for canals through which the boat most frequently passed. Some boats on the Oxford Canal would have O.C. followed by a number. Ovaltine had the number alongside the registration number.

Between Halesowen on the B.C.N. and the London Docks there were as many as 14 toll offices. For this reason every boat had a 'ticket' drawer up against the bulkhead by the stern doors for toll tickets so that they were close at hand.

Fig. 57. The steamer Phoenix *being gauged at Buckby.*

Chapter Six
Decoration

One of the most outstanding visual aspects of the narrow boat was its bright decoration; the cratch, cabin, interior and also the mop, bucket and tiller, were painted gaily in primary colours. The origin of the painting is not known; some ascribe it to the gipsies who

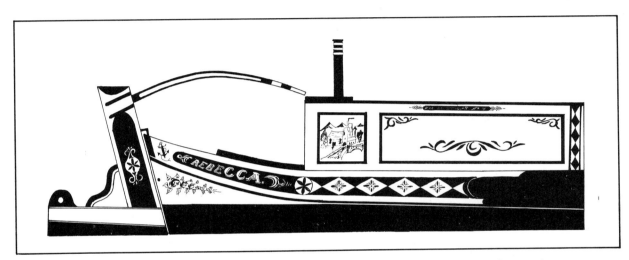

Fig. 58. Shows the general layout of the side of a butty boat. The following sketches and photographs illustrate the alternatives which can be used for the different sections.

Fig. 59. Polesworth lettering

Fig. 60. Polesworth roses. Note the leaves are shaded from left to right and the fine petals to the front of the rose. Polesworth (of Lees and Atkins boatyard) had symmetrical roses similar to Jones's but fluffier. Polesworth would paint virtually anything: cabin blocks at the Coronation with kings and queens.

Fig. 61. 'Knobstick' style table. This style was found in the north-west generally; there was also a boatyard with the name. The symmetrical castle is set in front of a bright orange sunset. The stylized roses can clearly be seen. Sometimes 'knobstick' would include horses and dogs on dipper bottoms.

happened to be in Manchester when the first narrow boats were built there. Inside, the cabin was full of hangings, grained wooden panelling, lace-edged plates and more paintings. The subjects depicted on a narrow boat were predictable: castles and roses were favourite, with occasional idiosyncratic varia-

Fig. 62. A stool and water can by Jones illustrating one of his fine castles. He did not always paint single-arch bridges – some have none, others have double arches.

Fig. 63. A horsebowl by Frank Jones, showing a good array of daisies and marigolds. He was lavish with his daisies, but the shapes were eccentric. The marigolds were wildly idiosyncratic, joined by bunches of roses.

Fig. 64. Jones castle.

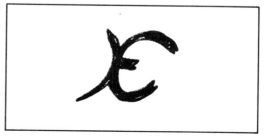

Fig. 65. Jones lettering. This kind of scrolly script was used for the middle row when there were three rows of lettering.

tions. The Shropshire Union Company, for instance, had stags on its boats pictured in magical landscapes, and some northern boats would have a cottage and church instead of a castle. Wall and Co. painted a brick wall on the sides of their boats and Chas. Nelson, who ran cement boats, had a cockerel on the cabin block and sometimes in the castle panel. Ernest Thomas had a diamond shape; Blue Line had a yacht wheel. Ovaltine boats bore the maid with her basketful of corn (who can still be seen on tins of Ovaltine); Willow Wren Canal Carrying Company painted their wren in a circular emblem on the sides of the main panel and sometimes the cratch, and the Cyclops Iron Company put a large eye in the centre of the cratch.

The artists who painted the boats became famous, and some of their individual styles are illustrated here; boatyards also had identifiable styles.

Fig. 69. A stool by Jess Owen of Charity Dock, Bedworth. Charity Dock specialized in daisies on long stems.

Fig. 66. Painted at William Thompson's boatyard, High House, Weedon.

Fig. 70. Faulkners, Leighton Buzzard.

Fig. 67. Painted by Yarwoods for Associated Canal Carriers.

Fig. 71. Fellows Morton & Clayton.

Fig. 68. Painted at the Anderton Company dock for J. & G. Meakin Ltd.

Fig. 72. Anderton C.C. Co. painted by A.J. Lewery.

Fig. 73. Jess Owen castle.

Fig. 79. Polesworth castle.

Fig. 74. From a stool by Jones.

Fig. 80. Jones's daisies.

Fig. 75. Design from the bottom of a Jones horsebowl.

Fig. 81. A Jones rose.

Fig. 76. A rose by George Crowshaw, who worked for Nurser.

Fig. 82. A rose by Jess Owen of Gilbert Brothers, Charity Dock, Bedworth.

Fig. 77. A knobstick rose.

Fig. 83. Polesworth rose.

Fig. 78. A Thomas Clayton rose.

Fig. 84. An edging by Jones.

Fig. 85. Jess Owen's daisies.

Fig. 86. An edging by John James.

Fig. 88. Nurser castle.

Looking first at the butty: on the outside of the boat, the cabin sides consisted of one large panel bearing the carrier's name and a small panel at the stern bearing a castle. Sometimes a third small panel was added at the other end of the large panel. Before the turn of the century, the big panel would usually be black, bearing the name or initials of the carrier, and the small panel, bearing a number or set of numbers, would indicate the canal registration number and fleet number. Lettering was an important part of the decoration, and was usually in serifed capital letters – white on

Fig. 87. A pair of Fellows Morton and Clayton boats near Watford. The main panel with the carrier's name and the small panel with the relevant numbers can be seen. Note the fine dress of the boatwomen.

Fig. 89. Seddons, salt-producers, did not aspire to a castle – they had a star motif.

black, black on white, with perhaps blue shading. Two-coloured shading was used with dark for the underside and light for the sides. The serifs sometimes might be curved instead of straight. Lettering in the case of a boat which did not have rectangular sides was a problem: the artist would use a strip of wood bent into a curve, and paint along this. The main surround to the panels would be white; if the butty's name was carved into the plank it

Fig. 90. Anderton C. C. Co. registration number.

Fig. 91. Severn and Canal Carrying Co..

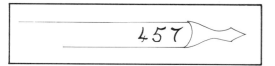

Fig. 94. General.

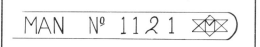

Fig. 92. Cowburn & Cowper.

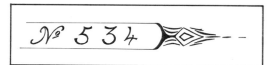

Fig. 95. Faulkners of Leighton Buzzard.

Fig. 93. J. Harry Taylor's boatyard at Chester.

Fig. 96. Castle by Polesworth.

Fig. 97. The anchor which is painted at the stern.

Fig. 99. Plain lettering of Thos Clayton.

would be black on white; if not, it would be white on a black band, with a white border. The rudder would be white, with coloured relief.

These rules of colour slowly changed – changes mainly being wrought by the Number Ones. Fellows Morton and Clayton chose for their livery, after the advent of diesel, red, green and yellow: revolutionary at the time. In 1934 the Grand Union Company used two shades of green, and later still the British Waterways had a smart blue and gold.

Before the lettering was put on, the panels were painted in bright colours; then the edging was painted. The Shropshire Union had fancy edging round the registration number panels of their boats; J. Harry Taylor of Chester put even more beautiful shapes on the boats of Arthur Sumner Ltd, millers and corn merchants of Wrenbury. Another handsome boat was owned by Joe Skinner, the last Number

Fig. 98. Lettering in gold leaf by Bushell's yard.

Fig. 100. A very good example of a Barlow butty; note the scroll beside the name, anchor, ropework, brass plates and the overall style. The fine castle was painted by Frank Nurser.

Fig. 101. Anderton C.C. Co.'s Shad.

One to trade regularly with a horse-boat on the Oxford Canal; his boat, *Friendship*, was bedecked by Tooleys at Banbury. The registration was usually painted in white on a black background just above the main panel. In the spaces left on the panel by the lettering would be the inevitable rose or perhaps a scroll. At the very stern of the name panel was a white space, which was traditionally filled with a slanting anchor with a large, coiled rope (usually dark blue or black). Below the name panel, the rubbing band was blue. If the panel tapered, a triangle was formed under the rubbing band below the loaded waterline. This was painted red and allowed to run up to follow the line of the boat – painted with roses or daisies.

Rudders were painted in a variety of ways, generally in a geometric fashion. The tiller, which was eight-sided, with four wide and four thin sides, might be in the two colours of the company's livery. Where the eight sides

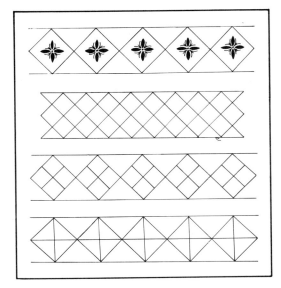

Fig. 102. Various lozenges.

Fig. 104. Stern doors.

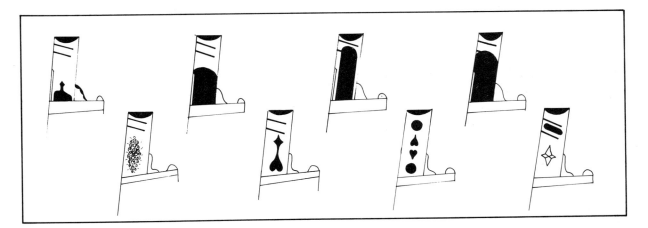

Fig. 103. Rudders.

tapered into a circle, the effect was like a barber's pole. Sometimes lozenges were painted on the wide side, or the name of the boat, with perhaps a small bunch of roses at the neck of the tiller.

The small stern deck was painted usually in the same colours as the stern doors, which were red in the centre, green on the outside, with a curving yellow band coming to an apex with the doors closed; the cabin was either red or grained. Graining varied according to the yard: Nurser's was always light, while Gilbert Brothers, Charity Dock, Bedworth, produced very dark – but very good – graining. The effect of graining was achieved by applying first a light-coloured paint, and then using on it 'scrumble' (wood-coloured, thick paint that came in various colours). After the scrumble

Fig. 105. A collection of boats at Brentford just after nationalization. Note the lining on the stern doors.

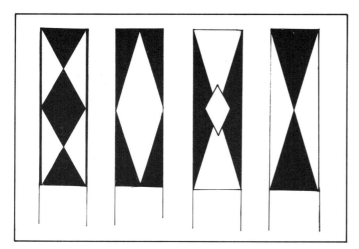

Fig. 106. Masts.

was applied, a cardboard comb was dragged through it so that the light undercolour showed through. Often a row of lozenges was painted down the centre of the cabin top; the hatches were painted white, with either a red club, circle or heart, bordered with green. On horse-boats, the mast stands and cratch were tall, and the stern plank curved round to the cabin block, the curved section being covered with lozenges. The stands and mast were painted as shown in the accompanying sketches.

Up to now we have only described butty boats; on the motor, the engine doors were often made of steel; if they were made of wood, they would be panelled in the same way as the stern doors, but grained or painted only with geometrical designs. On the motor, castles were rarely painted; there was one large panel with the name of the carrier, a smaller panel on the side of the engine room bearing the boat's name and number, and then the engine room doors, which occasionally had roses in their panels. The counter was usually white; red at the bottom (except for British Waterways, which had blue). The tiller was either painted in four or five coloured bands, or a multi-coloured barber's pole. The rubbing bands were sometimes blue and the stern deck green, with the well section red.

Even when the boat left the dock, painted and finished, it did not come alive until the boatman added his own personal artwork. The motor boat needed a stern fender, and this was usually supplied by the boatman himself; it was hung so that it pointed up in the air. Sometimes a wooden motor would have a wooden block secured to the hull to support the fender from underneath. These were often black because they had been soaked in creosote, and might have a band of rope round

Fig. 107. Cratches.

46

Fig. 108. Interior cabin door decoration.

them as a contrast. On the butty, the boatman was very enthusiastic about his ropework. Just above the tiller socket would be a 'turk's head'; from the top of the rudder to the very back a swan's neck was attached, with a brass knob at the top; it was like a big stocking knitted out of rope, with a lump three-quarters of the way up. Sometimes a horse's tail was strung from the top of the rudder instead of the swan's neck. On both sides from the rudder pivot to a small hole in the stem would be hung a small sausage-shaped fender. This would stop the rudder being damaged when it swung round and hit the rubbing band. One coil of ropework was added to the bottom of the tiller, acting as a fender when it was placed on the cabin top. Brass was fitted in the corners at the end of the cabin, partly to stop the paintwork being knocked when stepping aboard, and partly to prevent chafing from ropes. A small brass angle or aluminium strip was sometimes fixed on the motor to stop ropes chafing the corner of the cabin. Brass strip was also sometimes fixed on the top of

the cabin doors, usually where hands went, and on the leading edge of the hatch and the recessed end of the hatch.

The black chimneys bore three brass bands at the top, a little brass handle, and a brass eye. Sometimes a brass chain would join the eye to the deck, but more often brass links would be used, reputedly from war-time haversacks, though some boatmen found factories with a stock of gas masks which had suitable brass links. Just in front of the chimney would sit the water cans, which were used for all domestic water, including drinking water. These might sit on a special board to save wear on the combing. The cans were decorated with roses, sometimes castles. They always had a band round the middle: castles were often

Fig. 109. The bows of a Samuel Barlow motor boat; note the method of sheeting-up, the wooden strips which act as fenders, and painted cratch, and the white ropework against the black tarpaulin.

Fig. 110. An Ovaltine motor, showing the brass work attached to the tiller, the fancy fender, and the open door. In summer, the doors were usually left open, showing interior decoration.

47

Fig. 113. A double castled water can by Jones. The boy on the right is the author in 1950.

Fig. 111. The chimney of A.C.C. Shad, *showing the three brass rings and the links.*

painted on the bottom; Jones had a castle either side of the spout. The bottom band was sometimes painted in stripes with the boat or

Fig. 112. Some boat-people were so proud of their paintwork that they covered it up to protect it.

48

boatman's name in the centre. At one time buckets were common, and would be placed just ahead of the water can, painted with roses, and with the rivet heads picked out in paint. The mop gave the finishing touch, painted like the motor's tiller, slanting up at an angle but placed on the handle of the water can. Three spliced side ropes would dangle down the side.

The cratch was coated with jet-black tarpaulin, two white bands of fireman's hose and several white bands of ropework. When not painted, the front of the cratch was usually light-grey canvas or was made into a 'bulk' as referred to previously. The lamp used to be a highly decorative oil lamp; more recently it has become a powerful searchlight.

Fig. 115. The large Northwich Flamingo *with a bulk (1969).*

Fig. 114. A collection of F.M. & C. boats; the cabin block on Quebec has a portrait on it.

Chapter Seven
Living on a Narrow Boat

The narrow boat cabin was a small, cosy place; it was decorated highly traditionally, painted gay colours and filled with ornaments in a typically Victorian fashion – lace-edged plates being predominant. But as well as its delightful appearance, the cabin served as the kitchen, living room and bedroom for the family. All the family possessions would have to be stowed neatly away, and beds folded up to form cupboards. As we have seen, when the motor boat towed the butty, the cabin inside the butty continued to be the main living area,

but there was an increase in bedroom accommodation – some of the family could sleep in the motor cabin.

The general layout of a butty cabin (and the cabin in the motor was the same) can be seen from the accompanying plan and drawing; basically the furniture consisted of a bed which was formed by folding down a cupboard door across the boat to fill the gap between the cupboard and sidebench. During the daytime this was folded up, although on some motors and tar boats (where there was no access to

Fig. 116. The result, 2 weeks, 23 castles and 16 bunches of roses later.

Fig. 117. Glimpse of a narrow boat cabin.

the hold) the bed was either immovable, or was left down by the boatman.

Sometimes during the day a plank would be placed across the gap as extra seating at the table. Being across the boat, the bed was generally not longer than 6 foot 6 inches whilst in some cases it was considerably less. The width was only 3 foot 3 inches – a very small double bed. In the early days of narrow boats men were generally of shorter stature, though more recent lanky boatmen had more of a problem. If a bachelor, he would sometimes sleep on the floor. The bed section was divided off by a bulkhead. Continuing aft there was a cupboard containing a large number of shelves for general storage. The lid of the cupboard folded down to form a table, below which was a drawer for cutlery. Next to this was the range, while on the other side of the boat there was a continuous solid bench boxed in with

Fig. 118. Inside, the lace-edged plates and brass work are dazzling.

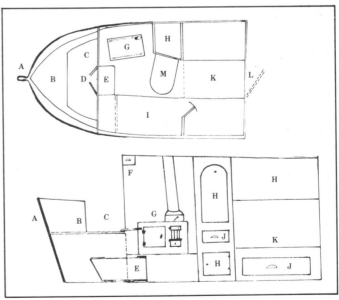

Fig. 119. General plan and side view of a butty boat living cabin.

A, Rudder Post.
B, Stern Cupboard.
C, Hatches.
D, Doors.
E, Coal-box & Step.
F, Ticket Drawer.
G, Stove.
H, Food Cupboard.
I, Side Bed.
J, Drawers.
K, Bed.
L, Door to hold.
M, Table.

51

Fig. 120. Looking down the centre of the cabin with the table lid folded down. The boatwoman is sitting on the crossbed which is divided off by the curtains at night.

storage space below. This was used as an extra bed as well as general sitting area.

Protruding inwards from the stern deck was a large platform which was used to stand on when steering the boat from inside the cabin, with one's head sticking out of the top. On the starboard side there was a bulkhead, the intermediate gap between this and the side of the cabin forming useful cupboard space, there being sufficient gap between the bottom of the cupboard and the sidebench to allow comfortable sleeping. On the other side of the boat, just under the deck, was a small ticket drawer for toll tickets, fags, matches, etc. A coal box was sited underneath the platform, the leading edge being used as an intermediate step.

When newly constructed, a cabin was pretty cold and dismal. The boatyard painter would then grain the whole cabin and various colours and paintings would be added. Then the boatwoman would go to work on her crochet hook, and finally crochet-work, lace-edged plates and curtains were hung round the cabin; carpets were laid, and the highly polished brasswork positioned. There was not

much likeness between this arrangement and a gipsy caravan but the whole effect was highly Victorian.

Much of the inside was panelled; originally the table top and sidebench were scrubbed wood. Many years ago a Jack Stove was used. The boatman, being conservative, changed to a range later than the land-based population – the range being the standard cooking equipment of any nineteenth-century kitchen. The boat-people were very keen on brass knobs, which were screwed on to every available surface, and always hung beside the door. They were identical to those on my grandfather's brass bedstead. The treasured lace-edged plates often bore the legend 'A present from ...' predecessors of the genuine English knick-knack made in Hong Kong.

There was nothing bizarre, strange or mystical about the layout, decoration and fittings of this small cabin; it was the centre of the family's life on a boat – a life that was insular, but not lonely. There were thousands of families on the canals, which had a high person to mile ratio. But progress did not affect the life-style on a narrow boat; as you stepped down on to the coal box you left the twentieth century, and saw life very much as it had been in Victorian England.

The range was the heart and soul of the cabin; the fire created the atmosphere with its pungent and distinctive smell and the omnipresent wisp of smoke from the very bituminous coal. There were two main types of range: the 'Guidwife' (pronounced as in any Glasgow tenement) and the 'Hostess'. The Guidwife was favoured because the tin oven could be replaced, whereas in the Hostess it was an integral part. The body of the range was polished black until it looked as though it had been stove-enamelled, while the edging parts shone like silver. The polishing was not just for aesthetic reasons; a range left in an unoccupied boat would quickly rust and look terrible. On the leading edge of the range and sometimes running round three sides was a highly polished brass rail on ornate supports, sometimes with an ornate twist in it. All round the back would be hung lace-edged plates with bright ribbons, miniature brass windlasses glistening on top of them, or maybe a row of ornate mugs which were more like jugs, all of which created a jovial, Pickwickian air. The pots and pans were compactly stowed on a shelf under the range which was neatly curtained off. Washing was hung on the copper or brass drying-rail suspended from the ceiling to dry over the ever-roasting fire. As one might expect, when the range was out, a neat cloth with a lace edge was placed on top with perhaps a couple of candlesticks and an ash tray. Others went one stage further and had a curtain which hung from the roof cutting the range off from the rest of the boat, presumably so it would not be splashed and get tarnished.

The most predominant characteristic was the fine detail in the cabin; the curtains had lace edges, every edge with a strip of crochetwork, and every recessed panel had a painted moulding. The floor was carpeted and a selected piece of wall-paper was placed on the step so, when soiled, it could be replaced. Out of crêpe paper large rosettes were made, and streamed from some of the plates.

It was in the evening that the cabin came alive; the double-burner brass oil lamp glowed, and the coal flickered, illuminating the rich colours of the roses and castles. The lace-edged

Fig. 121. *Looking towards the stern, showing the table in the up position on the right (the castle is painted underneath it).*

plates, with their white backgrounds, created an impression of light which one would have thought impossible from such a small light source. Cowburn and Cowper boats were reputed to have copper sheeting round the back of the range which would have enhanced the effect of the golden light. A favourite place in the evening was to stand with one's head above cabin level with the heat wafting up past one's face insulating it from the dank humours of the night. Smoke drifted vertically upwards, water voles went plop and silence reigned. What a shock a visitor had when the boatman lowered his table, and there was a portable television!

Cabins were kept surprisingly hot; generally

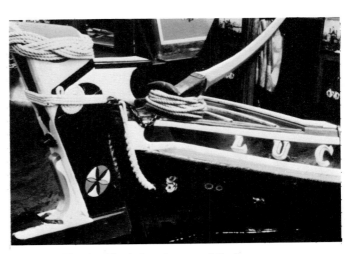

Fig. 122. *The freshly painted stern of the* Lucy. *Through the open door the curtain can be seen hanging in front of the range.*

53

Fig. 124. Brown leaves painted above the semi-circular table/door.

heat marks were evident on the ceiling above the range, and flames were occasionally visible coming out of the top of the chimney, especially at night and in tunnels. (Because of the danger of flying sparks, cabin fires were sometimes forbidden when moored near a wharf.) Yet on a cold morning the boatman or woman would appear with two overcoats standing in the boat and shout out to you on the towpath, 'It is mighty cold this morning.'

It is now time to ascend, via the coal box, back into reality and to reflect that at least in a house one does not normally have fifty lace-edged plates hung round a fire which have to be washed regularly as they collect the dust, as well as the endless brass to polish, black leading to shine, and a carpet to scrub.

Just a few notes here on the general interior painting: apart from roses and castles, there were some interesting geometrical designs, fancy edgings and dark brown leaves painted above the semi-circular table/door.

The motor cabin was very similar to the butty; with only the hull to the propeller under water, there was little storage space under the range and sidebench. The range, when the motor was working with a butty, was not used for cooking; sometimes a coal heater was substituted. The engine-room was clean and bright with all the copper parts of the engine brightly polished. Some boats had wooden panel doors to the outside; these were usually grained with geometrical designs, though most had steel doors. Cowburn and Cowper, whose boats were named after birds,

Fig. 123. Taken from a cabin door in the butty Virginis *(painted brown on graining).*

had polished metal silhouettes of the relevant bird on the doors.

The engine was always kept in spotless condition, the flywheel having a polished brass band over the top and all the exposed copper pipes glistened. Oil had to be checked and filled. Bolinders would spit out a fair amount of oil, which had to be carefully collected and disposed of as, when the boat was loaded, the bottom was level, and oil could seep into the hold, and in extreme cases discolour or damage bags of flour, etc. There was also the daily routine of bailing the boats out. In summer the planks would sometimes open out when the boats were empty and would take some time to swell closed. Steel and iron boats caused less bother. The motors often had mechanical bailers fitted to the engine but the butty would have a crude lift pump, the tube being in a wooden box either by the mast or by the stern end of the hold. When empty, water was often used as ballast in the motors to stop any cavitation.

The boat-people had their own traditional chinaware known as 'Measham', or, to the public, 'bargeware'. The china was not actually made at Measham, only sold there at a canal-side shop. It had a distinctive style which is best illustrated by the accompanying photograph. The boatman rarely bought any for himself but usually as a present for a special occasion such as a wedding or christening or as a 'thank you' gift, as it was much prized by land-based people who lived in other areas. If a boatman had been stranded because of floods or ice and had received hospitality, on his return he would give such a gift. This explains why in the late 'fifties examples were often found in antique shops in places such as Cirencester, Swindon and Wantage.

The following account from the *Birmingham Daily Mail* in 1875 shows how little the boat cabin has changed over the years:

'I have noted by this time the strange love of the boatman for pictorial display. He likes the outer shell of his cabin bedaubed in streaks of gay colour. Inside he rejoices in highly illuminated panels, he affects a gay pictorial pail, the top rim of which is embellished by a painted garland of small flowers; the body is enriched by designs of outrageous roses and sunflowers; while the bottom offers a good ground whereupon to depict a gay cavalier or valiant crusader in full armour. Any and every article serves as a 'ground' for the lavish display of the canal boat artist. If our water-faring friend has another weakness it is for knobs – knobs of all kinds, which he screws in everywhere. The dining-table cupboard-door is a very favourite place. I counted twenty-eight adorning one door; there were fourteen white china ones, six black ones, and eight brass ditto, and the combined effect was dazzling in the extreme.'

Fig. 125. Measham teapot; these are now collector's pieces.

Chapter Eight
Running a Narrow Boat

Despite the seaman's traditional scorn of the inland boatman's craft, running a narrow boat was not a simple matter. Even the loading required skill – different for each cargo. Coal fell off a chute into the boat below; timber, being an awkward shape, did not easily fit the narrow boat hold; bags of flour at Ellesmere Port bound for Wolverhampton would come down a chute and drop in the right place without handling. As the stacking progressed, the boat was moved so that the distance between the chute and the stacking area was at a minimum. The correct loading of the boat ensured that it would be trimmed properly (i.e. would be level), and therefore would steer straight. Some boatmen preferred their motors to be loaded slightly bow-heavy, so that when under way, with the stern dropped further into the water, the boat was level. In a butty, allowance had to be made for the buoyancy of the cabin area.

During unloading of flour a similar system in reverse was adopted: the sacks were pulled up by a rope through overhead hatch doors, the sidecloths being uncovered simultaneous-

Fig. 126. Loading the butty boat Argo *at Preston Brook with salt for export in 1970.*

ly. The ropes were always laid in the same direction and the cloths would almost roll themselves up because they were always done up in the same way. Surprisingly, one man could unload forty tons of felspar (a flint-type material carried from Weston Point to the potteries for china-making up to early 1969) by hand in four hours. At larger factories unloading gear was provided for coal. The jam hole (the wharf of Kearley and Tonge, jam-makers) at Southall had a small grab crane, but most of the coal traffic on the Southern Oxford was unloaded by hand.

Cargoes such as flour, wheat, etc, had to be covered up when the boat was under way. The arrangement was generally as follows: the top planks would be laid continuously along the tops of the masts and stands and along to the cabin blocks. At intermediate stages supports with 'V' ends would be wedged between the gunwale and the top plank to keep it in position. The sidecloths, which were firmly fixed to the gunwale, would be untied. On one side the top edge of the cloth had ropes attached every few feet. The corresponding cloth on the opposite side had an eye. The rope would be cast over the top of the plank, through the eye on the opposite cloth, pulled tight, brought back over the top of the plank, and tied back onto itself. It was never tied too tightly in dry weather as canvas shrinks when wet and might split. At this stage, the hold was only covered halfway up the side, the canvas dipping between each rope. From the bow locker were produced four large top sheets; these were laid over the top plank and sidecloths, and almost reached the gunwale on both sides, the overlap was so large. The sheet in the bow, which had been folded neatly into the cratch, was then folded back to reveal a hole which dropped over the mast. As a final precaution against leaks, a small strip was run out along the top plank just astern of the mast. This strip, for some reason, widened out by the cratch. All the topcloths were held down by lines which passed right over the top,

Figs 127 & 128. A pair of Birmingham & Midland C.C. Co. boats loading coal on the Ashby canal.

between eyes fixed into the gunwale. Cargoes like coal, especially where it was going to be stacked in the open at its destination, did not need to be covered; but because of the low freeboard, sidecloths only would be used, or sidecloths from the bows to amidships as, in a lock, this was the area most likely to be affected by water from the gate-paddles. Some boatmen would not put all the stands up and the tension in the topstrings would make the top plank arc down; other boats used to use no sidecloths or topcloths at all. There were sometimes variations in complete sheeting up; there could be a step in the mast with shorter stands the same height as the cabin top, or, where timber was concerned, no stands at all, but the whole hold sheeted over, giving a barrel-like appearance.

One short cut was to have topcloths with an eye in each corner to secure them, thus eliminating all the top strings, but these would fairly flap around in bad weather.

The boatman showed the extent of his ingenuity in the way he took a pair of boats through a lock. To begin with, a third member of the family or crew (known as the 'lockwheeler')

would cycle along the towpath to prepare a lock for the coming boats. Even here he would take short cuts: for instance, if the lock was full, and the boat going uphill, a paddle would first be wound in the bottom gates to assist the closing of the top gates, and he would skilfully stand where the gates met and push the far gate open with his foot, thus saving a walk right round the lock. Apart from the appearance of a man riding down the towpath, the coming of a boat some quarter of a mile or

Fig. 130. A stop to roll a cigarette during unloading a pair of F.M.C. horse-boats in Manchester, 1922.

Fig. 129. Motor boats unloading bags of bentonite (a kind of mud used in well-drilling) in Wolverhampton; note the side strings hanging near the chimney.

more away could be told by the fast movement of water and a faint throb from the engine. There were many squabbles about precedence at locks when boats from opposite directions arrived simultaneously; a method was evolved whereby two posts were erected equidistant either side of the lock, and whichever boat passed the post first had precedence. If the lock was full, the boat going downhill had precedence.

On a downhill trip (wide lock), when the lock was full, the boats were slowed by the water pushed before them; the motor was easily stopped by its own power. When the paddle on the bottom gate was drawn, the steerer only had to give a gentle push to the balance beam on the top gate and the rush of water slammed it shut. The butty was stopped in one of several ways: sometimes by a rope from the bow to a bollard near the bow, which was done when the lockwheeler was required to stop the boat if his wife was unable to leave the boat. Another method was to use a thick rope which was attached to the side of the butty near the stern around the bollard at the entrance of the lock, and then finally round the ground paddle post (see Fig. 136). Generally with this method the line trailed in the water during the summer but was coiled on the cabin top and looked rather untidy during the winter. The most ingenious method was where the boatwoman leant over and passed a line through the hand rail of the gate and back to the stern cleat, thus closing the gate at the same time as stopping the butty. The final method was to connect a rope between the motor and the butty and stop them together as they came into the lock.

Once in the lock, paddles drawn and gates shut, a line from each boat attached to their masts would be taken to the respective bottom gate. Each line would pass the gap between the hand rail and tie in a slip knot against one of the uprights, such that when pulled in one direction it would hold firm and in the other come free. When the lock was empty, the motor would go astern, pulling its gate open. As it started to go forward, the butty would automatically move back, thus opening its own gate, and when in this position the butty was held back by a line attached to the top gate, as otherwise the butty would tend to stick to the motor as it came out of the lock.

Fig. 131. Unloading by hand on the Thames & Severn Canal at Brimscombe Mills.

Fig. 132. A mixture of joey & narrow boats unloading coal at Hawkesbury power station.

Fig. 133. A pair of Harvey Taylor boats enter Berkhamsted lock on a cold, wet winter day in 1951.

Fig. 134. The butty being held back in the lock while the motor goes out.

As the motor moved out of the lock, the gate opening line would automatically undo itself and either fall on to the hold or trail in the water. As the motor picked up the butty's bow rope, the line holding the stern would be shaken free.

This sounds, in explanation, a very laborious, complicated task, but in practice, it was executed with the utmost speed and dexterity, and the whole operation was done to the busy rattle of paddles, clonking of the gates, creaking of ropes, and throbbing of the engine, which usually had rather a slack governor so that at tick-over, the engine kept slowing down and then picking up for a couple of beats; this was particularly noticeable with the single-cylinder, slow-revving engines. With

Fig. 135. A pair of boats pull open the bottom gates.

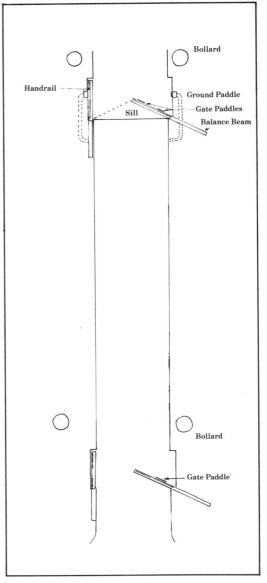

Fig. 136. Diagram of wide lock.

these engines, especially when the boats were empty, the whole motor would twist (on boats with wooden hulls) at the same time as the planks jumped. Rings were formed on the mug of tea on the hatch, can lids chattered, and articles on the butty's folding table slowly jumped nearer the edge.

Similar techniques were used on the uphill journey. On entering the lock, a top paddle was drawn; by the time the boats were touching the sill, the paddles were fully drawn, the butty, if not breasted up, had no difficulty in getting in as when the motor was in gear a circular current was formed in the lock. The

Fig. 137. A boatman polishing his brass chimney, while travelling along a lock-free section of canal. In front of him is a 'pigeon box' (not used for pigeons, but for ventilation to the engine room).

boatman shut the gate on his side by putting his tiller hard over and forcing a jet of water between the gate and its recess. This forced the gate closed enough for the general flush of water to close the gate.

When the lock was almost full, the bows would bump over the sill and ram the lock gates, pushing them open a little, but the head of water would send them back into place. Just before the levels were equalized, the motor was taken to the back of the lock and a charge taken at the closed gates, forcing one open, and the butty's bow line was picked up on the way out.

Similar procedure was adopted on narrow locks, where boats had to go through singly. (A narrow lock is nominally 7 feet wide, and a wide lock is 14 feet.) On going downhill, the butty was cast off to allow it to slow down. The top gate was given a small shove to close. Most narrow locks have double bottom gates

so with one open and one closed, a mere step was needed to bridge the gap. The top paddle wound speeded the exit. At the bottom of the lock a short boat-hook was used to give the balance beams a prod, and these indentations can still be seen on many old wooden beams. The water coming down the lock chamber shut the gates.

By then the lock was almost full, and ready to receive the butty. When the lock was empty, with the butty in it, the motor, which had been left in stern gear, outside the lock, would automatically open the bottom gates and the pair would then proceed on their way. Similar operations were gone through on the uphill journey. The boatmen on the tar boats *Tay* and *Leam* would sometimes go through this operation single-handed on the Napton flight on the Southern Oxford. Occasionally, a long eighty-foot line would be used by the motor to pull the butty into the lock. Usually

Fig. 138. The boatman's answer to wet weather was to arrange a hood over the steering position.

on flights of locks which were very close together the butty would be pulled by hand between the locks, while the motor went on ahead. At one time canal companies or carrying companies had their own horse or horses at a particular flight to assist the butties. On the narrow canals much single boating was done and where there was only one person it could be difficult in very deep locks such as Middlewich, since the boat was so far below the ground level. When going downhill at a deep lock, a line was taken out to keep the boat to one side of the lock, the engine would be left in gear, and the bow kept on one of the two gates so that, when empty, first one gate could be easily opened, then the bow would be pulled across, the other gate opened, and the boat would come out by itself.

The boatman's day started early: that is, any time from 4.30 a.m. On hearing a passing boat at 2.45 a.m. one never knew whether it had been running all night or had just started up. However, in the early years most locks and toll-houses were closed at night and also on Sundays. If the boatman was in a hurry he might tip the lock-keeper to open out of hours; the practice was recognized by the canal companies and some even laid down the amount to be tipped – on the Trent, Beeston Lock cost 6d (2½p), and on the Erewash, Trent Lock cost 1/- (5p). When railways became competitive with the canals, all-night working came into force; the Sunday ruling was also weakened, since railways ran seven days of the week.

The first jobs on rising were to see to the fire, start the engine, and get going; followed, quickly, by a cup of tea. This was often a perfect time of day; while waiting in a lock the air was calm, the smoke, which was always thick, streamed vertically upwards; the water was still, the morning light shone horizontally into the cabin, showing the brass and paintwork to its best advantage. Often four to five hours later the sky would become overcast, the wind begin to ripple the water, and outboards would start on the transoms of small white cruisers. The boatman, who had already covered what would be a good day to the pleasure boater, would become irritated when he had to wait at locks.

Boat-people lived by rigorous routines; they were so familiar with the canals that they set themselves targets to reach each day. Because they knew the routes so well, they would plan their schedules minutely; when there was, say, half an hour's gap between locks, the brass could be polished; there might be a three-hour gap in the locks tomorrow so the washing could be done. The lockwheeler, too, had his itinerary worked out, and between locks would divert via such and such a shop which they always patronized. The boats never stopped during the day; meals were taken on the move, usually in rotation and rarely on the cabin top in public. Eating times also were predetermined by the occurrence of locks.

Brass was always polished daily, along with the mopping down of the paintwork. The hold was cleaned after every cargo – a thing that would only be possible with a good routine. Morale was maintained by the necessity of keeping to a schedule; many amateurs have, for example, found themselves bogged down by what seems an interminable number of locks in the section of canal from London to Cowroast on the Grand Union; traversed in a single day they seemed easy.

Steering was always done with a nonchalant air, and the boats never got stuck, even when loaded, on shallow canals. Being so long, the tiller had to be straightened before the boat had finished turning and the handling qualities of the boats were very variable. Small Woolwich, for example, had a small counterbalanced rudder in front of the pivot and no effort was needed to move the tiller, while others would need strong arms when trying to turn at full throttle. When steering, the boatmen always stood within the cabin doors and only on the stern deck to let someone in or out of the cabin. In summer, the fire was allowed to go out after about seven or eight in the morning. Wearing perhaps a collarless, pin-striped shirt, cuffs rolled, exposing bronze arms, sometimes in the heat of the day the boatman would sit on the cabin top with his legs dangling through the hatch. He would not spend much time with his hands on the tiller; it was vaguely moved by his back, his arms and his sides, and only on sharp bends would his outstretched arm grip the smooth wooden handpiece that was always attached to the end, as metal would be too cold to touch.

Life would finally come to a halt between eight and nine at night, often at a popular place. Pairs would, for instance, tie up at a pub at Great Linford, which due to lack of trade no longer exists. Other favourite pubs were the Greyhound at Sutton Stop, the Crystal Palace at Berkhamsted, and the Red Lion at Preston Brook.

Even though much navigation was done in the dark, the headlight was little used except for entering bridges and locks; I have seen the *Halsall* and *Banbury* make a perfect job of going through two locks and a swing bridge breasted up without a single light. By not having a light there was no glare from the slight evening mist and shapes could be quite easily discerned; the boat-people knew every bend and every turn. Boats were navigated in thick fog, and, even when the bows were out of sight, the boats kept moving, as the boatman knew exactly how tight and which way the next bend was and what revs were needed to

Fig. 139. The motor Chiltern *continues to work north through thick fog although the bows can barely be seen.*

Fig. 140. A pair of empty boats pass through some major repair works. The cross-over of the towing lines, as described in the text, can be seen.

navigate in the deepest channel.

On one occasion a newly married couple were both standing in the hatchway navigat-

Fig. 141. The ice-breaker at Great Linford in 1895.

ing through Birmingham in the dark without a headlight and with their minds preoccupied they forgot about the toll island in the middle of the canal!

Various arrangements were used when towing the butty. When empty, two very short ropes were used with eyes spliced at both ends. The bow of the butty was brought tight up into the motor stern fender. One rope went from the cleat on the butty round one side of the bow, the other on the other side. They then crossed over and each went to a cleat on the motor (the motor having a cleat on each side). In this manner, the butty was virtually self-steering, and its tiller could be held straight by the two eyes attached to each side of the hatch being slipped over the end. A similar arrangement was used for the motor when in a lock to stop the tiller from swinging and hitting the side. When loaded, either a medium or long line was used; in recent times it was attached to the bow cleat, where once the running block via the mast would have been used. Generally, the shorter line was used in locky areas when travelling between locks, and the long line used only on long pounds, although boatmen seemed to have their own preferences as to the length of line. The butty was always steered slightly to one side of the motor so that the full force of the propeller did not strike the bow. The boatman would always slow the engine when approaching a narrow bridge and then rev up when he had once entered it, otherwise the piston effect (water resistance slowing the motor down) would have stopped the motor but not the butty, which would have rammed it smartly in the stern.

During summer holidays many people have envied the boatman's job but the admirers are few and very far between durinng the winter

Fig. 143. The horse-drawn boat Dorothy being towed through broken ice on the Trent and Mersey canal.

months. At one time ice-breakers were numerous. They were pulled by as many as twenty-six horses and broke the ice by charging at it, either by direct impact or by sending a tidal wave which would crack the ice some distance

Fig. 142. To avoid delays, a pair of British Waterways narrow boats which have been iced in are unloaded at Barbridge Junction.

Figs 144 & 145. Four tugs and five horses pull a string of narrow and wide boats along the Paddington arm through Greenford, Alperton and Sudbury on Tuesday, March 5th, 1929. The tug shown in detail is the Powerful *owned by Thos Clayton (Paddington) Ltd.*

that the boat was swayed with greater vigour and without anybody feeling cold.

The boats were constructed of wood with very fine lines so that they could run up on to the ice and then smash through. The timbers were of fantastic proportions and one wonders if making a dug-out would not have been easier. More recently, diesel-driven steel boats did most of the work, but with the suck-down of the engine, impact speeds were not as great.

One of the best-known incidents was the sinking of the ice-breaker (or 'ice boat' as it was sometimes known) at Stockton. After a four-day battle against ice in 1939, twenty-two pairs of boats reached Wigrams (Calcutt 3, as it is known to most people) from Braunston. The ice-boat took a hundred-yard run at the ice, and ran half out of the water on to the ice. The horses were stopped and the boat slid back and sank. The boats waited six weeks in the ice until they were relieved by an ice-breaker from Birmingham.

One problem with ice was that it would wedge boats in locks. In wide locks the boats

ahead. All this was accompanied by rocking of the boat by a large gang of men to help smash the ice. One of the most celebrated captains used to insist on his crew being half drunk so

would go through separately, but in narrow locks the ice was pulverized with 'podger' bars. It has been known for boats to be 'left hanging' in a narrow lock when they have been wedged by ice. In cold weather, boats carrying perishable goods would always tie up at night by wharves or places of easy access so that their cargoes could be transferred to road if necessary.

In more recent times the boats were left to break the ice themselves. When thin, it was broken with no trouble and with no apparent drop in speed, to the accompanying sound of breaking glass. As the ice became thicker, it was harder to steer as the boat tried to follow the path of the cracks in the ice; the impact of hitting large lumps of ice could be felt and the

Fig. 147. One of the few remaining Bushell-built boats was an ice-breaker built for the Grand Union Company. Now used as a work boat by T. Harrison Chaplin Limited, it can often be seen on the Thames.

Fig. 146. A Birmingham tug does its own ice-breaking while towing joey boats.

propeller heard chewing the solid ice. As conditions worsened, the butty was unhitched and the motor charged forward. For ice-breaking the Woolwich were superior to the Northwich boats although in one more recent case, where finance was tight, a Woolwich boat had to stop, for, as she went astern before taking a run at the ice the clay puddle (the impervious clay used to line the canals, which in this case was used to fill a gap in the counter) was being pushed out of place by the ice. Metal always sheathed the bows of wooden hulls, and occasionally a thin strip covered loaded and unloaded waterline near the stern, so that boats could continue in safety during ice. Ice scored wood very badly and without protection the boat would have leaked by the end of a trip.

In cold weather, the range was always alight. The stomach was kept warm by continuous cups of tea. The hands were either dangled below hatch level in pockets, or warmed on the chimney. The wife would complain that she could not scrub the butty cabin top as the water would turn to ice and make it dangerously slippery to jump onto, despite the small mat placed on every cabin to soften the tread of the boatman's heavy boots every time he landed from the lockside. As night drew near the frost began to have more vengeance. A hoar would start to build up on the cabin over the engine and along the top planks. There was no walking to the bow to jump off at a lock and the bow-deck was treated with great caution as it became covered by icy water when the gate paddles were drawn. The boatman had to be surefooted at night as the gates, too, were icy and a good grip was needed on the hand rail. Ice had to be freed from behind lock gates to open them.

The boat-people worked very extensive hours for minimal wages, and it is not surprising that there was a steady drain from the boats to the land towards the end of trading. Yet many land-based boat-people still talk of their early life with nostalgic memories perhaps of working fifty-two hours non-stop and having to splash one's eyes to keep awake ... - Many families had never travelled on more than a couple of routes but when the boatman had once moved to a house, he felt homesick for his favourite stopping places and his feeling of freedom. Even when they did settle, many ex-boat-people returned to the canalside, where they could still watch, talk and ramble along the towpath.

Chapter Nine
The Boat-people

Boat people were an insular community. Firstly, this was due to illiteracy, which made them feel self-conscious when they were ashore; secondly, the public attached to them the stigma of being water-gipsies; thirdly, during this century they worked unusually long hours which did not allow time for socializing in the towns through which they travelled. In practice, they usually shopped in the same stores and the shopkeepers, for example in a village like Braunston, would know them and respect them. Because of their isolation from people on the land they were very conservative, and their way of life became almost anachronistic.

The great meeting-places for boat-people were the canalside pubs. Many of these were run by ex-boat-people and dealt almost exclusively with the boat-people. Some of these today are still well known canalside pubs, now frequented by canal holidaymakers, but many others have closed. A good canalside pub would have stabling for horses to attract boat-people to moor there at night. The pub would not only be a place to exchange gossip, it also provided an opportunity for entertainment. The boat-people would bring their musical instruments and have a sing-song, to which someone would usually get up and tap-dance. Tap-dancing was a traditional accomplishment, and even the clumsiest of boatmen were agile at the steps.

Business would also be conducted at the pub; people would look for work, buy and sell boats, horses and brass ware. All sorts of transactions took place there; the publican provided facilities for special purchases and

Fig. 148. A boatwoman aboard the Florence eyes the photographer with distrust.

Fig. 149. Boat-people having an evening chat at Hawkesbury Junction while Barlow's freshly painted Lucy passes through the stop lock.

also for cashing cheques, and was, therefore, an important link with the outside world.

The following description from the *Birmingham Daily Mail*, March 12th, 1875, gives a different impression:

'The canal-side town "public" is a thing to be remembered. You come on it suddenly, hiding modestly in a dark hole or corner of a dark wall. Its dirty little windows display weird and fearful compounds; its sign hints in irregular printing "ale, porter, cider, and tobacco," and being "drunk on the premises." I go – of course at another time without my kind guides – to inspect the amphibious "public." I find the grimiest of low-ceilinged taproom, a truly savage and barbaric "tap" wherein is dispensed the thinnest and flattest beer I have ever yet come across. This is the "bargee's" usual tipple, for rum is only a special for great occasions. Greasy wooden "settles" and battered wooden tables furnish the apartment, and there come the "jolly bargemen" to make merry. The walls have two distinct and clearly defined rows of black lines, indicating the presence of greasy backs and heads, and when the boatmen have mustered "harmony" reigns. I can give no better idea of one of these taprooms than by referring the reader to that bit of word-painting by Dickens, and etching by Cruikshank, "Scotland Yard." The ballads peculiar to boatmen possess either the humour of the not specially decorous country ditty, or the sentimentality of the Holywell-street "lay" as retailed in fluttering half-penny tissues pinned to ragged sheeting in "shy" corners. Occasionally the younger boatmen launch out into a sadly garbled version of some flashy music-hall song, but this is looked upon rather coldly. The singer having duly rammed his hands deeply into his breeches pockets, leans his head against the wall, fixes his eyes on the ceiling, assumes a most serious and dismal countenance, and goes to work with the air of a man doing penance for his sins. The choruses are frequent and tremendous. The "harmony" is often relieved by a little step dancing, in which, strange to say, the boatman is an adept; the big burly men are wonderfully light of foot, and keep time accurately. The orchestra is usually composed of a fearfully dilapidated old man, operating feebly on the last remains of an ancient fiddle, and extracting thence wheezing old jigs and ghostly strains of nigger "breakdowns." I confess that I incline to look with much horror on the boatman's "public." These places are so retired and hidden that what can be easier than a little quiet drinking within prohibited hours, or keeping open later than Mr. Cross approves of? They are nasty, suspicious dens, to say the least of it, and I fear, that the over-refreshed "bargee" is by no means a lamb when he gets home to his unfortunate family.'

Many boat families, in fact, had what they called a home town. For example, a boatman working for Faulkners of Leighton Buzzard who principally carried sand from Leighton Buzzard to various parts of the country would probably feel Leighton Buzzard his home base. In the same way, people working for Harvey Taylor of Aylesbury whose main trade was to and from Aylesbury would feel this their base, and people in the salt trade would feel their base was in Middlewich. Often generations of boat-people worked for the same firm or in the same area, so a boat family would retire to the land and buy a house there, and in turn the next generation would moor their boats up there because their parents or grandparents or aunts and uncles lived there. Whenever there were marriages or deaths the trips were arranged to coincide at this spot, and if a woman was expecting a baby, although in the old days they tended to work right up until the baby was born and the boats just stopped for a very short time, an effort would be made to reach there for the confinement. In the south the favourite stopping-place for such occasions was Stoke Bruerne, where Sister Mary Ward lived in a large house beside the top lock. Sister Mary Ward devoted her life to looking after the boat-people; finally she was awarded an O.B.E. and also became a subject of 'This is Your Life'.

Many theories have been put forward about the origins of the boat-people, most of which try to associate them with gipsies. The late L.T.C. Rolt has been one of the proponents of this idea, and he connects the boat-people with the gipsies who lived in the Mosses of Manchester, near where the first canal, the Bridgewater, was built. He also links boat-people to gipsies by their art and their dancing. However, I believe otherwise; the canals took

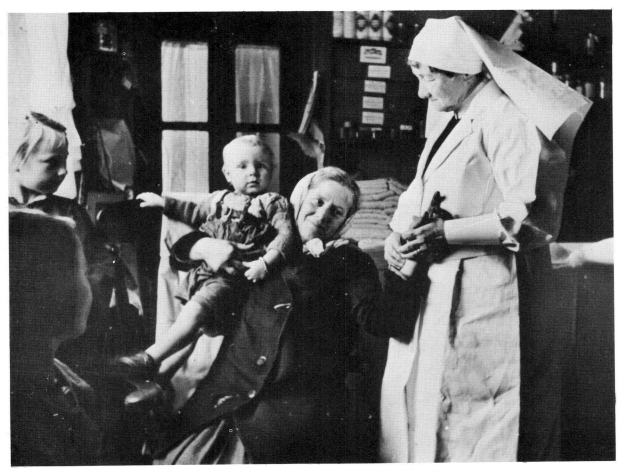

Fig. 150. Sister Mary Ward conversing with a boatwoman and her child.

many years to build and so there was ample time for the canals to find recruits from society as any other trade.

Though the railways were not the immediate cause of the phenomenon, the predominance of family boating coincided with the growth of railways. With horse-boats, company bye-laws usually ruled that the boat be steered by a man over eighteen, and the horse led by a boy over twelve. With the two boats travelling together, the wife was a partner in running the boat. It was usual for the boatman to steer the motor while his wife, traditionally referred to as 'me mate', looked after the butty. Although this was a slightly easier job, she also had to prepare meals and look after the children at the same time. Vegetables would be prepared in a dipper (a bowl with a handle) on the cabin top, while under way, with an eye kept on the range below. The boat-woman, from the range, produced delicacies from roast pork to castle pudding.

Children learnt at an early age that if they threw things out of the boat there would be no kindly Father Neptune handing them back on the end of a three-pronged fork. They would disappear for ever in the oozey mud. Young children were strapped through an eye on the cabin top so that they could not wander over the edge and similar precautions were taken on the side bench in the cabin. When empty, the door leading from the cabin to the hold was opened and the children would tear up and down on their bicycles and tricycles. A line could be strung between the masts to accommodate a long string of washing without the fear of it being soiled by coal dust, and the carpets and rugs for some reason always appeared to be airing on poles laid between the crossbearers. Washing was not always carried out on a Monday but was always conducted in the butty cockpit, in a large galvanized bucket. These buckets had a large lip at the bottom which fitted exactly over the top of a giant Primus. The clothes simmered for several hours, producing a whiter-than-white wash.

71

In addition to all her housekeeping, the wife was expected to get off and help at every lock. As a young girl she would have been expected to assist her parents to run their boats, often helping to bring up younger brothers and sisters. If she was the eldest daughter of a large family, pressure was often exerted on her to marry to relieve the accommodation problem, whereas an elder son often worked on the steamers.

Unlike her land-based contemporaries, she was deprived of continuous courtship because, unless by coincidence her boyfriend was travelling in convoy, they saw very little of one another. Along with the majority of boat-people, she would be illiterate and so did not even have the consolation of private love letters. The toll clerks would often help to write and read the letters, which were invariably decorated with flowers and perfumed – usually with violets. A common sight was initials with a heart and an arrow formed by paddle grease graffitied on to the white balance beams of a lock gate. Few had the looks or the wit to marry outside the cut and once married there was little time for romance with long working hours, and a husband in sight but often a hundred feet away.

The furnishings of the inside of a narrow boat cabin were predominantly the influence of women. It was they who collected lace-edged plates and made the crochet-work and

Fig. 151. A boatman closing a lock gate in London; note the flat cap, waistcoat and belt.

collected the trimmings. With the low wages, the boats had to keep moving and with young children this could be a problem; even for a confinement a boat would only tie up for a couple of days. Though the men were the captains of the boats, on a couple of occasions their widows have taken on the running of the boats.

Before the railways, the fly trade on canals was very important. By tradition, this was a round-the-clock male crew activity. This tradition was transferred to the steamers and later it was the bachelor with mate with a single motor who continued the fly boating. One reason for single boatmen being used for these trips in the early days was that a lot of work was short-haul; the boatman would live at home, only spending the odd night aboard, and wages were relatively higher to afford this extra accommodation. But when the railways cut the time of journeys, it was the fly trade that left the canals.

Boat-people were generally looked down upon by the land-based community, even though the boatman had a much better standard of living than many land-based people. The first factory act was not passed until 1801 while the Earl of Shaftesbury's Acts were not passed until 1833. The latter made it unlawful to employ children under nine and allowed children of thirteen to work no more than nine hours a day and forty-eight hours a week. Boy chimney sweeps continued until 1875.

Another problem for the boatman up until 1812 was the press-gang; whenever they approached dockland, it was common practice on Thames boats for young captains to exchange boats with old men.

From about 1825, when railways began to compete, narrow boating was in decline; I believe this bound the community closer and made the traditions stronger. Boatmen knew that there was no chance of wages being improved and this made them feel that they had been rejected by society and ignored by bureaucracy. Many a time a pair of boats would be tied up at a factory and have to wait while the lorries were served first, making them feel second-class citizens.

Boat-people had their own moral code – not the same as ours, but perhaps stronger. No one would lock his boat cabin when he moored at a place like Sutton Stop, where there were other

Fig. 152. A mother and child aboard a butty while waiting to load.

boats around; they had complete trust in the other boat-people. However, they also assumed the right to use the cargoes they carried (no boatman ever bought coal when it was available from the hold) and to poach on the property they passed. For this reason, mooring beside some parks and chases was not allowed. Their feelings of comradeship sometimes extended to giving a bag of coal to a retired boatman. It was unusual, though, for boatmen to pilfer more valuable cargoes. On one occasion, a boatman delivering a load of sugar slipped down a gap between the sacks and carefully inserted a small tube into a sack to draw off some of the sugar; unfortunately by so doing the bags above toppled over and crushed him to death.

Poaching was really one of the boatman's hobbies. There was never any feeling of guilt, and, as one boatman put it after an unsuccessful prosecution, 'My back garden stretches from London to Manchester.' Generally, the shot was fired from the boat and the boatman's dog would jump off the cabin-top, swim to the bank, collect the quarry and bring it back to the boat at the next bridge-hole. At other times the boatman leading the horse would keep a look out for prey. The boatmen liked such delicacies as moorhen's eggs as well as all the general game animals. Sometimes vegetables would be taken from farmer's fields.

Another of the boat-people's hobbies was gossip; passing boats would exchange the latest news about others on the cut. As the butties drew apart in opposite directions the boatwomen developed shrill voices to help prolong the conversations. Because of the

73

Fig. 153. A pair of boats moored in the country.

large amount of gossip, each family felt it was imperative to maintain tight schedules and a spotless cabin.

Though wages declined in the nineteenth century, the quality of life aboard was still good. The boatman had freedom within the job in that, provided he met the overall time schedule, he was his own boss. But the greatest advantage was having his wife and family with him all the time. You saw young boys being taught how to handle a boat by proud fathers, and in what other job could one have a cup of tea every half hour? Work, home and pleasure merged into one. Boatmen find it difficult to adjust to a nine-to-five environment, without their families. Boat-people lived a healthier life, passing through wonderful countryside, never shut up indoors.

The craft moved at just over walking pace, slowly enough for travellers to observe the animals and the countryside, and when tied up often the doors were open or people stood with their heads out of the cabin.

The proud and self-respecting boat family was as well turned out as its colourful boat.

At one time men invariably wore corduroy trousers, always pale coloured, usually white. One lady now living ashore recalls that her father had three pairs of cords and wore a clean pair every day – it was her job to scrub them! The boatmen's trousers were unusual in that they had flaps rather than flies. Men's shirts, like women's blouses, were voluminous; a typical shirt made by a boatwoman used four yards of cloth and one yard of calico lining. The ultimate in shirts was a Sunday best, embroidered down the front with lozenges matching those on the boatman's cabin. Fancy braces with a needleworked spider's web design were *de rigueur*. Men's headgear was either a flat cap or a black bowler, and, of course, women were proud of their bonnets, made from some three yards of material. For every-day, boatmen tended to use thick leather belts which made ideal windlass holders, and invariably they wore waistcoats. The ladies had long dresses and aprons. In the south, heavy hobnail boots were commonly worn, and in the north, clogs. There was the heavy Lancashire clog, a native of the Bridgewater Canal, the

74

Cheshire clog, which was made in a small corrugated iron building by the entrance to Barnton tunnel on the Trent and Mersey Canal, and finally the dainty Shropshire clog, a native from Ellesmere Port. Much of the clothing in the South was made at Penningtons of Brentford.

The boat-people celebrated Christmas in much the same way as everyone else. As Christmas approached, each family tried to adjust its speed of work so that it 'just happened' to be at the desired place – near the rest of the family – by Christmas Eve. A bunch of holly or a Christmas tree would be tied to the rudder post, and the Christmas fare would be obtained beforehand. One particular boatman used to have his bow locker full of game and would sell to other boatmen.

If a boatman died on his boat, he would be carried 'fly' back to his 'home' village for burial. It has been known for coffins to be slid across the frozen canal as the only means in severe weather of getting the corpse to its destination.

One of the few pieces written about the boat-people appeared in *Life on the Upper Thames* (Virtue, Spalding and Company, 1875) and is reproduced below:

'We have used the word "barge" as being the most familiar term; "canal-boat," "monkey-boat," and "wusser" are other names for this description of craft; but the people actually concerned always speak of it as a boat.

'The spotless neatness of the little cabin, and the last polish bestowed on the brass fittings, are characteristics they frequently have in common with the pleasure-yachts of our upper circles. It seems that only on the water can one learn how brilliant a polish brass will take. The exterior decoration of these boats is noticeable, and evinces the pride taken in their appearance by the owners, who repaint them with the gayest colours as often

Fig. 154. In contrast: the potteries.

Fig. 155. The late Jack James dressed in traditional costume with embroidered belt and braces, flat cap and neckerchief.

as they can afford to do so. On the outside of the cabin are painted two or four landscapes (usually river-scenes), of which they are proud enough; and it is curious they invariably speak of them as "cuts." ... The smartness of the cabin part of the barge is often the more striking, from the fact that the load it bears is of a very opposite character, as coal, which is perhaps the most common freight. Thirty tons is about the average weight one boat is capable of carrying.

'We have mentioned the fact that these boatmen pursue the same line of life from generation to generation. From what cause we know not, but they are remarkably exclusive, in daily life mixing as little as possible with the villagers with whom they come in contact. They are a class apart, and have an undisguised contempt for the ordinary rustic, chiefly, as far as we can gather, from the fact of his clumsiness. They say, with some truth, that unless a man is born and bred to boating, he is never lissom enough. It may be only the assumption of superiority usual with *travelled men*. In return, as is but natural, they are disliked by the villagers, who class them with gipsies, laying the blame on them for ducks' eggs missing, or damage done anywhere. Their

spirit of independence, amounting to a general readiness to fight, is a marked contrast to the opposite manners of the peasantry, especially noticed by Oxford undergraduates, between whom and the "bargees" there is an old-standing hostility. A few families marry and intermarry, much in the manner of an old Scotch clan. They have preserved by tradition the old-fashioned belief in the medicinal value of many herbs that are now discarded from the pharmacopoeia. By their travels they become acquainted with the spots where the herbs are to be found, and occasionally collect them for sale in the towns through which they pass. Agrimony, and what they call thousand-leaved grass (probably yarrow), are the most in request. In reply to our question as to what they were used for, we were always told, "to make tea of to take when you're ill;" we never heard anything more specific as regards their application. When these remarks originally appeared in the *Art-Journal*, we had stated tansy, and not yarrow, to be what was probably meant by thousand-leaved grass. However the *Lancet* honoured our statement with some interesting annotations, from which we extract the following: "The herb known as the 'thousand-leaved grass,' so much valued by the bargemen of the Thames, is the well-known *Achillea millefolium*, common yarrow of milfoil. It was highly valued by the ancients as a styptic vulnerary and astringent. John Gerard, known as 'Old Gerarde,' in his 'Herball' of 1597, says: 'The leaves of yarrow doth close up wounds, and keepeth them from inflammation or fiery swelling.' It is, in fact, one of the favourite remedies of the bargemen and common people throughout England, Scotland, and Wales, and is applied by them universally, externally as well as internally, for almost every ailment to which they are liable.

'The common charge brought against the barge-people, that their language if often unfit for ears polite, is, we must allow, too well grounded to be refuted. Their customary style of expression is decidedly more energetic than elegant. In palliation, we would ask our readers what would be thought of a country gentleman of the present day who should talk as Squire Western did? And bearing in mind how the class we are speaking of has kept to its own circle for generations, we can account for their retaining language which may be partly

76

Fig. 156. A boatman and his wife returning empty up the Nene after unloading grain at Wellingborough, 1961. The boatman is wearing the usual cap and waistcoat and the brass buckle at the back of his belt can just be seen, while his wife's dress would not have looked out of place in the 'thirties.

set down as the fault of a past age, with which they have so much in common.'

Finally, this description of the boat-people would not be complete without a tribute to their charming character; although shy to outsiders, they were by nature warm, open people and to those whom they accepted, they were constantly helpful and courteous. When passing on the canal, each family would wave and exchange greetings.

The Canal Boat Acts

Mr George Smith of Coalville (1831 – 95) was one of the great Victorian philanthropists. His first success was improving the lot of the children employed in the brickyards of England; his campaign aroused the interest of the Earl of Shaftesbury, amongst others, and resulted in the passing of the Factories Act (bricks and tileyards) Extension Bill in 1871.

In 1873, Mr Smith turned his attention to the canal population. He wrote letters to the press describing the squalid and overcrowded conditions in which boat-people lived. The following extract from the *Leicester Daily Post* of April 27th, 1874, gives an example of his first onslaught into the lack of education and overcrowding:

'The condition of the boat children was something alarming. He was talking to a respectable looking woman the other day as she was going into her cabin. He said he would like to make a few inquiries of her, and she invited him into the cabin to look round. He found everything in apple-pie order. On asking her how the children were educated, she exclaimed, "Edecated, man!" "Can any of them read or write?" he asked.' "Read or write, man! no! I can't understand how it is other people's children are 'scholards' and ours are not 'scholards.' Others get looked after and edecated, but ours are not. I wish some one would take up our case." The boat children were far, far worse off than the brickyard children, because they were constantly floating up and down the rivers and canals. The sailors left their children behind them, and some kind friends in the town looked after them, but it was not so with the boat children, who were constantly moving, altogether uncared for – as they were, so they are, and to all appearance would be, unless something were done to benefit their condition. If they looked at other classes of workpeople, tailors or colliers for instance, they found men had risen from the ranks and made their way in the world, but whoever heard of anyone from the boats becoming eminent in any walk of life? His object was to amend this state of things. And was not this a work in which Sunday-schools ought to take a part? He heard that sometimes as many as two hundred boats lay at Moira on a Sunday. Where did the people from those boats go? did they stop on the banks? Were there Sunday-school teachers at work amongst them? Oh! it was a Sunday-school work, and they ought to do all they could to get the children and parents too, to go to

Fig. 157. The woman's dress and bonnet can be seen in more detail.

Sunday-school. He saw a boat the other day in the cabin of which there were only 202 cubic feet of space, and living in it were a man, his wife, and six children, one of the girls being 16 years of age, one 14, a youth of 10, and so on. A man, and his wife, and six children, and only one room for everything! Those of them who had families knew what that meant. He asked the woman of whom he had first spoken how she and her husband and the children slept. She showed him a table in front of the fire, and said three children slept on that, two lay under the bed where the parents slept, and two in a little cupboard above. The height of the cabin was only about five feet. It was not right that such a number of people should be stoved up in such little space – no wonder at fevers, and all kinds of diseases – but it was so. In one boat he saw the other day were a man and woman and two children, in another a man and woman and three children, in another a man and woman and five children, in a fourth a man and woman and four children – he was sorry to say he could not call them all wives in those boats.'

The Daily Telegraph of the August 7th, 1874, ran a leading article condemning the size of the cabins:

'A statement made by the excellent Mr. Smith himself, at the meeting at Polesworth, will show the difficulties with which the subject is surrounded. He said that he had recently brought under his observation the case of a woman who, during the last twenty years, had not slept in a dwelling-house. She had brought up a family of eight children in a cabin, containing not more than 202 cubic feet of space in which must be included stove, seats, cots, and kitchen furniture, so that it must have borne a remarkably strong resemblance to a rabit-hutch. One of her children slept at the head of herself and her husband's bed, another at their feet, two in a cupboard, and the remainder "where they could put them." As a rule, Mr. Smith added, our floating population are very dirty in their habits, and degraded by their mode of life; but he admitted that there were some whose cabins were clean, who conducted themselves respectably enough, and were a credit to their employers. Let us supplement the admission by stating

Fig. 158. Boat-people having a morning wash, which would have delighted Mr Smith.

that a large number of bargees are thoroughly respectable, and that many of them are frugal, and in time become substantial men. These are the "boaters" who lease their barges from the owners at a fixed rental, and, in process of time, save enough money to purchase the craft outright, or to have a new one built for themselves.'

A sad accident at Newcastle-under-Lyme was reported in the *Staffordshire Times* of May 15th, 1875, which added weight to Mr Smith's argument:

'On Tuesday morning an inquest was held before Mr. Knight, at Newcastle-under-Lyme, touching the death of a little child, aged three months. He was the youngest born of George Millard, a boatman, who, at the time of which we write, was stopping at the Lime Kiln Wharf. It is usual to state in such cases the residences of the unfortunate bereaved: but where is the residence of our "floating population?" Let optimists view them and answer. They are, as a general rule, in a box, for we can hardly in justice call such places *rooms*, placed in the bows of lighters. Perhaps one of the most repulsive scenes in any of Marryat's novels is that which is included in the first or second chapter of *Jacob Faithful*, namely, an account of the hero's birthplace – a lighter. It

Fig. 159. As he so rightly says, some cabins were damp ... In the background is a loading shute for iron ore at Blisworth. This was carted down the Northampton arm where it was smelted.

makes one think of the temptations, of the miserable times, and of the fearful ends which some of this class must succumb to. We had no opportunity of inspecting the homes of the Millards, but we have learnt enough to know that it was no fit place, either in size or characteristics, for the six beings confined in its walls. A father and mother and four young children made such a place – which we are assured was not more than four yards square – their home. One morning this home was anchored, as we have said, off the Lime Kiln Wharf. The whole family were assembled in their one bedroom. On one pallet were stretched father, mother, and the deceased, the latter of whom was recognised by his mother to be alive at four o'clock. When she again woke, she found another of her children, aged about nine years, stretched over the head and body of her youngest born, who was discovered to be suffocated. The unfortunate cause of this fatality appeared to have got up from his bed, and for warmth or other cause, placed his head down by his baby-brother's. Sleep suddenly overpowered him again, and he

awoke at his mother's call, the unconscious cause of his brother's death. The inquest resulted naturally in a verdict of "Died from suffocation."'

The next wave of attack was directed at the question of spreading diseases; it was well covered by an article in the *Leicester Daily Post* on September 3rd, 1875:

'Adverting, in the first place, to the physical mischief which this curiously-dangerous floating population may, and undoubtedly does, spread abroad in the land, we need only instance the cases quoted by Mr. Smith of "a boatful of typhoid fever;" of small-pox and other fever patients and dead bodies carried about from place to place in the suffocating cabins of the boats, with the manifest risk of infecting healthy localities. We hardly dare follow our informant into this unsavoury part of his subject; but all that he advances will readily be understood when taken in conjunction with the following quotation: – "Small-pox and fever and the two principal diseases the boaters suffer from. They *wash and cook with, and in many cases drink, the water of the canal.* A medical officer in his report to a Town Council a few weeks ago said that in the canal passing through the town "the water was inky black, and the stench was intolerable. Large bubbles of gas were continually rising to the surface, being unmistakable proof of decomposing animal and vegetable matter." This will refer to all canals passing through or close to our large towns; so thick in many places are dead animals floating on the surface, that the "boat-gauger" has to push them out of the way before he can gauge the boat. This is sowing the seeds of disease with infernal effect, and it is in this atmosphere "our floating populations" have to live.'

Many articles appeared decrying the cruelty which the boatmen imposed on their families and the teaching of foul language which largely stemmed from the drunken stupour in which they lived. Like many Victorians, Mr Smith was strongly motivated by religious fervour. But he sensibly realized that the distribution of Bibles was pointless to an illiterate society. He did have the grace to admit that some boaters lived in exemplary fashion, as he wrote in the *Birmingham Daily Mail* on March 12th, 1875:

'In happy contrast to this slovenly den is the next boat. A hale, ruddy-faced old man comes tumbling up the cabin steps to bid us enter, and "have a talk to the old woman." We clamber from boat to boat, stoop low, and enter another cabin. It is of the same dimensions as the last, and has the same lockers, cupboard-door, table, &c., but it bears in its tidiness and order the sure signs of a woman's hand. The brasswork and tinware is in the highest state of polish; some huge plated candlesticks – family heirlooms, I presume – the night lantern, the brass knobs on

Fig. 160. A pair of Number One boats with a family aboard. Closer observation shows the wealth of painting. Note how the rudders and tillers are tied together.

cupboard-doors, &c., all glisten again. The old man descends, and seats himself by the side of his smiling, tidy old woman, and they look as confortable an old Darby and Joan as you could wish to behold. Some gay scraps of fringe decorate the beams of the bed place, and framed mourning cards of deceased relatives are hung about. For twenty-eight years these good folks have known no other home, and are, they say, quite happy in this floating ark of their declining years. They own the said ark, too, having bought it out of hard-earned savings. This is often the acme of the boatmen's ambition. The value of a boat is from £100 to £130, and with care it may last twenty years. These good people trade mostly to Worcester and the Black Country, and are paid by the "trip." Both are – when in port – constant attendants of the "Bethel," and we leave the model couple spending quite a pattern Boatmen's Saturday Night.'

Fig. 161. Mr Chapman dressed up as Father Christmas delivering gifts to boat-children.

One very fair comment appeared in *The Sunday at Home* in 1878. The whole crux of the argument really depended on the proportions of boatmen in the categories described.

'There are three classes of boatmen: 1st. Those who work what are termed fly-boats, and who travel night and day, changing boats at various places on the road, carrying goods of the best kind and most urgently wanted. Three men work one of their boats, and can earn sufficient to keep their families comfortably at home, no women and children being allowed on board the boats. 2nd. There is the old-fashioned boatman and his family, whose father and great-grandfather were boaters. Many of these may be considered honest and trustworthy, carrying flour and other valuable goods, earning good wages. The best of this class have to get along, as best they can in competition with the "Rodney boatmen," perhaps earning about fifteen shillings per week, after all expenses are paid. 3rd. The "rodney," "loafer," or third boatmen, in nine cases out of ten are those who have run away from home as youths, because work put too severe a strain upon their disposition, and begin to loiter about the stables and hang about the boats, occasionally driving the horse for a few miles, to get a "crust of bread and a glass of grog," and in this kind of work going on from one thing to another, till they get a piecemeal employment, as "helpers" for perhaps a dozen different masters during a month, doing the dirtiest work for a mean pittance, spending their days in drunkenness and wretchedness, to the injury of themselves and their fellow men, and lowering the respectability of this kind of labour in every possible way.'

Mr Smith was obviously campaigning for the latter. For the following ninety odd years the distinctions between groups 2 and 3 remained.

The result of Mr Smith's campaign was the passing of the Canal Boat Acts, 1877 and 1884 which enforced the following points: the boats had to be registered by a local authority who laid down for each craft the number, age and sex of people who were permitted to sleep in the cabin; all boats had to bear this registration number on the side of their cabin. To halt the spread of infectious diseases sanitary authorities were given powers to stop boats from travelling to other towns when infection was aboard. The Act also tried to tie the responsibility for schooling to the local authority with which the boat was registered. In practice this was very difficult to implement especially with younger children who were not old enough to attend a boarding school. Some of the canal companies had attempted to improve education amongst the boat-children, but their efforts varied widely, and were usually linked to religious teaching: in 1839, for instance, the Oxford Canal Company voted £20 to a floating chapel for boatmen, which also carried on board a schoolmaster and schoolmistress; the Staffordshire and Worcestershire Company also gave money to the Boatmen's Pastoral Instruction Society, and the Weaver Navigation in 1840 built three churches and established schools for canal children. British Waterways also later opened schools at key points. But all these attempts at education only gave the children a smattering of knowledge, since none could overcome the problem of the children being constantly on the move.

The large number of boats with bow cabins as well as stern cabins is pictorial evidence in

Fig. 162. The Salvation Army's butty Salvo *moored at Braunston.*

the late nineteenth century of the working of the act. Though the aims of the act were worthy, it did not improve the image of the boat-people with the public.

Other charities adopted the boat-people; the Salvation Army had a pair of converted boats which traversed the Midlands. In the south the London City Mission opened the Boatman's Institute at Brentford; which did much for the boat-people of the Grand Union, under the leadership of Mr Chapman.

Chapter Ten
Horse-boats

On the earliest navigations, as on the natural waterways, wind-power was used to propel craft when available. When it failed, man-power was used, and even until the eighteenth century teams of men could be seen hauling boats. They did not even have the advantage of a towing-path, but had to scramble along banks and wade through shallows. Gradually horses – and sometimes mules or donkeys – took over; in the days of the horse-boat, one horse would tow the boat and, because journeys were so slow, the boatman and his family would live aboard the boat. By this time, towing-paths had been cleared; when, due to estate boundaries, the towing path had to cross the canal, a bridge was built so that the

Fig. 163. The boat horse 'Bonnie' has a quick feed from his nose-bowl. The arrangement of the harness can be seen.

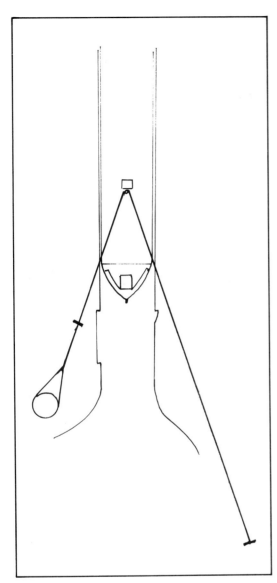

Fig. 164. A plan of the pulley arrangement as described in the text.

horse could cross. Narrow boats were designed to be propelled solely by horse or mule, but few are to be seen now; towards the end of the nineteenth century steam tugs began to be used – though mainly on fly traffic, where the benefits were greater. Steam-drawn boats were not much faster than horse-drawn, but the engines did not need to be changed as frequently as the horses on a fly run, where they were changed every four hours.

Horse-boats were the same as the present-day butties, and they even worked in pairs sometimes with just one horse, although this was more common on wide canals such as the Grand Union. It was usual for one family to keep the same horse in the way they kept the same boat. Each horse had his own characteristics: some would side-step, which necessitated adding a link to one side of the harness which meant a quick change by adjusting the link at roving bridges (when the towpath changes from one side to the other). Before nationalization, the Shropshire Union Canal ('Shropie') was very shallow and the horses were very timid at bridges where the towpath swung round towards the centre in case the slowing boat pulled them into the canal. At this time, the towpath on the Shropie was constructed of white chippings and Thos. Clayton used to fit their horses with shoes which had a few protruding teeth to help give them a good grip, while on the B.C.N. the paths were covered with ashes.

It was customary for horses always to drink canal water. In fact, on the Shropie there were only a couple of taps on the whole length for the use of the boat-people. Often Birmingham Canal water was not suitable for equine consumption, so a large number of taps were provided for their use. In cold weather, the boatman would rub his hands in the horse's bucket of water to heat it up.

Several devices were introduced to help the horse when starting to pull a stationary boat; the most common, used mostly when starting out of a lock, consisted of a long length of rope with a large eye at one end with a toggle (wooden peg) inserted some twelve foot from the tip of the eye. When the boat was in the lock, the eye would be dropped over a bollard ahead of the lock gate on the opposite side to the horse and the line brought to run through a pulley on the mast (this would give the horse a two to one mechanical advantage), until the mast was almost level with the bollard, at which time the toggle would stop the rope passing through the pulley. The horse was then under normal load. The boatman or woman would then unhook the eye off the bollard and jump aboard the boat.

On the Shropshire Union, horse-boats were towed on an eighty-foot line and, because of the difficulty in getting through bridges, sometimes one of the boat-children would jump ashore and knock in a stake just ahead of the bridge and use the pulley mechanism just described to help the boat through the bridge.

Fig. 165. A horse pulls the Clayton tar boat Rea *out of a Shropshire Union lock.*

In a similar way, motor boats would always cut their engines when passing a horse-boat on the Shropie so that it did not judder to a halt on the bottom as the motor sucked the water away from under it. Empty boats gave way to loaded, which meant that the rope had to be passed over the empty boat; it was easy for Clayton's as being decked there was nothing to catch the ropes on.

It was a marvellous sight to watch a horse-boat in action. Coming into a lock, the horse instinctively knew when to stop pulling, and, because of the absence of engine noise, the creaking of the rope wrapped round the bollard to stop the boat could clearly be heard. As the lock filled the horse became impatient to get going and would look round, waiting for the signal to go.

When under way, the boats had good acceleration and glided through the water, travelling better than a motor because a motor-boat propeller sucked the water from under the hull making it harder for it to move. A good horse would ease up on approaching a bridge and in low bridges turn his head sideways so that his ears did not hit the roof. Some horses were tunnel-shy, and one remedy was to have the boat on a short line so that the horse was

within the beam of the headlight. Horses for canal use came from various backgrounds; 'Bonnie', who worked with Fellows Morton and Clayton's *Dorothy* trading regularly on the Trent and Mersey, had been a circus horse in the nineteen twenties and used to amuse the boatmen by giving a display of tricks. It is said that some of Fellows Morton and Clayton's horses came from Arabia and were tethered for three days in Ashted tunnel by the first lock to get acclimatized.

Horse-boating meant that the majority of tunnels before the advent of the tugs had to be 'legged'. This meant a plank was laid across the bow deck and two people would lie on the plank, one at each end, and put their feet against the walls of the tunnel and 'walk' the boat through. Usually the plank was, in fact, two separate short planks with a large hook at one end which went through an eye on the foredeck. Various lengths of plank would be kept depending on the size of the tunnel being legged. At some of the major tunnels there were gangs of professional leggers who would charge a set sum for taking the boats through. In the case of just a husband and wife working a boat where there were no leggers, the wife would take the horse over the top of the

Figs 166 & 167. A joey boat is pulled up Farmer's Bridge flight in the centre of Birmingham. The horse-bowl can be seen on the hatch. The man leading the horse is moving forward to pass the tow-rope over the lock gear.

tunnel and the man would take the boat through by shafting it. The shaft had a large wooden cap at one end; the boatman would stand in the well, put his shoulder against the cap, the other end on the bed of the tunnel and propel the boat by pushing on the shaft, similar to punting. It is interesting to recall how Thos. Clayton always purchased their shafts, forty at a time, from Rathbones dock in Manchester, although most of their boats were built in the south.

During bad droughts the Tring summit of the Grand Union Canal used to become so short of water that horse contractors were called in to help pull the boats through or over the bottom and down as far as Fishery Lock, Boxmoor. One sad event was when one such horse with a nose-bag attached fell into the canal and drowned. Had a conventional canal horse bowl been used, he probably would have been saved. An account of the drought was given in the *Daily Mail* on Tuesday October 7th, 1902.

'Between Marsworth and Boxmoor, on the important canal which connects London with Braunston and Leicester, there are fifty pairs of barges waiting for water to float them through the locks.

'This block is the worst effect of the drought in Hertfordshire and Buckinghamshire. It is causing serious delays in the London supply of all kinds of merchandise – coal and ironware from the Midlands, new corn from some of the arable counties, condensed milk from Aylesbury – and in the Midland supply of sugar, tea and other commodities in bulk from London. Heroic exertions on the part of the Grand Junction Company's engineer and servants do not enable more than eighty or ninety barges a week to pass over the Tring summit, whereas in times of plentiful water one hundred and thirty pass.

'It was on the Chiltern Hills above Tring that surface wells gave out soonest, and this trouble with the canal traffic began five or six weeks ago. As the canal falls on both sides, water for locking purposes must be provided by hook or crook at the Tring summit. There are one hundred and one Locks.

'An extraordinary meeting of boatmen stretches three miles along the bank and never adjourns. Their horses lie down and go to sleep, their wives sit knitting and gossip, their children playing in the fields. It is good fun for the youngsters, this being a fine season for

Fig. 168. The horse 'Nigger' pulls a Fellows Morton and Clayton boat through Armitage tunnel, known to the boatmen as 'Plum Pudding' tunnel. It has since been opened out to form a cutting.

nuts and the blackberries ripe. Their elders are not so well content, because boatmen are paid by the journey: but, like the company, they make the best of it. You may see them sitting picturesquely grouped sometimes for a "sing-song." They are supposed to get an occasional rabbit for the pot.

' "Strike me lucky, it's a picnic, sir!" said one

Fig. 169. 'Bonnie', the ex-circus horse, performs one of her tricks outside The Swan at Fradley.

of them, "Never 'ad such a time in the country. All we want is free baccy an' a band, wiv fair pay for listenin' to it".

Forcing a Passage

'But day and night at the locks, very slowly, the double stream of boats mounts or decends, while more accumulate. There is just enough water not to cease working.

'Along the summit level it is low. A steam barge grounds upon the muddy bottom and snorts vainly; it is necessary to yoke a couple of horses on and thrash them into helping off the engine. Struggles of this kind are incessant, and the company's depreciation fund will feel them.

'Two large reservoirs at Wilstone and Marsworth are running dry, and soon there will only be mud for the hundreds of wild duck which haunt them. A pumping-station at Cow Roast, that draws from the lower chalk, is labouring with a reduced head of water. Once before, in a summer drought, water was pumped up at great expense all the way from Braunston, lock by lock; but this year Braunston has only water for its own needs.

'It is the pumping station, brought into use two months ago, that has saved the traffic from cessation. Even before this began to work the Bulburn river was dry from Dudswell down to Crooked Billet; one might have walked on it for two miles. Such want of water in October is not remembered in either county. Wells which have never failed till now, tapping the great sponge of the Chiltern rock system, are exhausted twice a day to supply the shortcoming of shallower ones.

'Berkhamsted, desperate, accuses the Canal Company of the whole mischief. The Hertfordshire County Council is admonished of a duty to stop the water of the district being drained away from it.'

On the Regent's Canal, recesses with grooved ramps can still be seen which were built to help horses climb out if they fell in, the idea being that the horse would walk along the bottom till he came to a ramp where he would be coaxed to climb out.

Generally, it was not too difficult to get a horse out of the canal (which was about 3 foot 6 inches deep); you knew that another boat containing some able assistance was guaran-

Fig. 170. Two boatmen prepare to leg a boat through Maida Vale tunnel.

teed to come round the corner within the next five minutes, and also, the towpaths were lined with telegraph poles. The procedure was to fit a block and tackle to the top of a telegraph pole, get the horse near to the bank, and lever him upwards with a plank under his belly, using a pile of stones for a pivot. Having been lifted so far, the block and tackle would be used to keep the horse high while he was swung onto the bank.

The old generation of boatman, in particular, treated his horse very well; always making sure that he was stabled, fed and made comfortable for the night before he would go into his cabin or the pub. Stables were sometimes provided by locks, or at pubs. When the towing horse could not be stabled, he was tethered on the bank by the boat. The horse was always regularly groomed, 'till 'e shone like glass', and some canal horses won prizes at local shows for the best turned-out horse.

The boatman would make sure the horse's collar was warm and dry before he put it on –

Fig. 171. A day boat travelling along the Coventry Canal to the Collieries. Note the crude mast that these boats used, and the boatman's dress on the right.

Fig. 172. Poor accommodation, but shelter from the rain for the tired horses.

as he would with his own socks. Along with the rest of the boat, the horse shared an array of brasses and had his own brightly painted horse-bowl and colourful bobbins. Sometimes each bobbin was painted a different colour, others would be painted in four colours like a barber's pole. Even the wife did not forget the poor old horse, and crocheted him a pair of ear-caps to keep the flies off in summer.

The division between horse-boating and motor boating partly was between generations; the horse boater was of the old school, whereas the younger generation preferred the powered boats.

Fig. 173. A boat horse receiving new shoes.

There was also more of a clannish atmosphere among horse-boats, and several boats or pairs, made up of relatives or close friends, would travel together. This would mean that they would have to wait at the bottom lock and again the first ones would wait at the top lock, but because of their age they had known more affluent times and did not need a mad rush to earn a living. In the same way, they expected to work long hours and would scorn anyone who stopped during the day even though they might have started earlier or intended to finish later.

Sometimes, wanting a quick exit from a mooring place, or wanting to be first at the next lock, the boatman would tie bags round his horse's hoofs so he would not disturb the neighbouring boats. A short time saved this way near a destination made the difference between being first and last to unload.

The horses travelled a fair distance. On a typical trip on Clayton's Ellesmere Port run, they did the following sequence: – Oldbury to Norbury junction (31 miles, 23 locks), Norbury to Chester (42 miles, 38 locks); and then Chester to Ellesmere Port, load and back to Chester all in the one day. At each of these places would be stables; a good example of stables is at Autherley Junction which is now a clubhouse and bar. Stables came in two standards: either general dormitory stables where the horse would be tied up for the night, or a private loose box. It was more often the older boatman who would put his horse in the loose box; his son would rather spend the money on an evening at the flicks, a bottle of beer or a packet of fags.

It was important that the horse was not overfed the night before a long journey, in case he were too bloated in the morning. A. and A. Peate of Maesbury Mill, Oswestry, had some very fine rugs for their horses, similar to those worn by racehorses.

Mules and donkeys were also used to pull narrow boats – donkeys usually in pairs. But they had to walk side by side; if they went single file the one in front had to keep stopping to see how his mate behind was getting on. It was sometimes awkward at bridge holes as the inner animal tried to push the outer into the cut, while the other tried to push the first one into the wall. Thus they went through the bridge in a 'V' formation. Many boatmen

Fig. 174. Thomas Clayton tar boats at Oldbury having just arrived from Ellesmere Port.

would lead the horse along the towpath; at other times the children would do it. Even this job would have its difficult points. A horse could force his handler into the brickwork at bridge holes and then scar his body by dragging the tow rope across his chest while he was trapped. Lazy boatmen would not walk with the horse, but send their dogs off at a bridge to bark at the horse to get him to pull faster. The horse was not just a method of power; he acted as an indicator of an approaching boat.

On the main line of the Grand Union the demise of the horse took place quickly with the introduction of steamers, the modernization of the Grand Union, the large new fleet of the Grand Union Company, and the awkwardness of the Braunston and Blisworth tunnels. On the lower Grand Union, Regent's Canal, Lea and Stort, etc, the horse-drawn barge continued into the early nineteen sixties when it was superseded by the diesel tractor.

The Shropshire Union Canal was entirely used by horse-drawn boats up to 1921 and was much slower in changing to diesel, while a few day boats in Birmingham have been pulled by horse up to, and including, the nineteen seventies. One of these horse-drawn boats still operates.

Horse-boating varied considerably from area to area. In Birmingham, for example, though the boat-people were all land-based, they always celebrated May Day. The animals were dressed with great care as the boatmen rivalled each other's horses. In the winter, they had mustard in the morning and stale beer in the evening to help fight the cold. Perhaps one of the most amusing stories was of the horse who found his own way to the boatman's house and knocked on the door with his nose-tin.

Chapter Eleven
Number Ones

The most notable horse-boat owners were the Number Ones – the owner boatmen. Number Ones in the south can be broadly categorized: first there were the large number who were employed on the carriage of coal to Croxley Mill from the Midlands. These boatmen in effect did the same trip year in, year out. Second, there were boatmen who traded mainly on the Southern Oxford (as opposed to the Grand Union), some having trade with one customer only, others carrying whatever trade was available. These Southern Oxford boatmen gave the canal a completely different atmosphere from the main line. The canal became a by-way with the opening of the canal from Braunston to London, and trade was therefore local. The canal linked both canalside and riverside market towns.

The Number One boatmen in their heyday carried the bulk of the traffic; Fellows Morton and Clayton rarely used the route. These boatmen therefore generated their own community and way of life, and, because of the smaller numbers, the community lacked the formality of the main line. The boatmen, of course, had to find trade. At Oxford there was a boatman agent who, for ten shillings (50p), would give a boatman a cargo. En route brickworks (such as Napton) and cement works would display a sign if they wanted a boat. At the colliery end there was, of course, no problem finding a cargo.

Coal was the main cargo on the Southern Oxford, although as late as the early nineteen sixties Willow Wren carried coal to Oxford, Samuel Barlow coal to Banbury and Thos Clayton tar to Banbury. Stone from Hartshill was transported to many of the canalside wharves for road making, and both the cement works and the brickworks generated much canal traffic. The Southern Oxford had many wharves and some can still be discerned. The biggest and best was at Banbury where the bus station now stands. The whole area round the small arm was stacked with piles of assorted coals.

The through traffic on the canal was mostly to Thames-side towns although some traffic was destined for the Kennet and Avon. Charles Nelson, who carried cement and operated steamers, gained a contract with the Thames Conservancy as a consequence of which they had one of the first diesel boats built by Nurser which had a kitchen rudder and was named *The Gamecock*. Their steamers were bought by a quarry at Hartshill who carried stone to the Upper Thames. One steamer had two butties on the long lock-free sections and horses were employed on the Lower Southern Oxford and were stabled at Duke's Lock while the steamers took the horse-boats in tow up river to Radcot, Tadpole Bridge and Lechlade. Eventually the steamers were sold to Faulkners of Leighton Buzzard who converted them to diesel craft. One of them, the *Jason*, eventually finished up, in the early 'fifties, with John James, who used her as

Fig. 175. A narrow boat tied up opposite Tooley's boatyard at Banbury, with a typical Oxford Canal bridge in the foreground.

Fig. 176. The steam boat Jason owned by Chas Nelson.

a tripping boat at Little Venice.

Number Ones were astute businessmen and looked for trade in which they could buy and sell and hence make extra money. Here their big contact was the pubs. Many canalside pubs were owned by ex-boatmen. It was here that the boatman's integrity was noted. The publi-

can would lend money if necessary and if a cargo 'backfired' he would store it.

Before the turn of the century, Number Ones would gather at Napton, where the ex-boatman publican also owned a field. Here the boatmen would meet, celebrate, and buy and sell horses and boats; the pub provided

Fig. 177. A canal stoppage like this meant no income to the owner boatman or to the employee, since he was paid by the journey.

Fig. 178. A horse crossing the Trent by ferry in 1931.

cooked meals to retain custom and add to the celebrations.

During his normal travelling, the boatman would keep his eyes open for suitable merchandise. For example, on delivering a load of coal to Sandford Mill a cargo of mangel worzels might be bought from a local farmer and sold to one at Wormleighton. The corn and hay merchants in Rugby used to frequent a canal pub and much buying, selling and transporting of hay was done to the town, mostly from Oxfordshire.

Fig. 179. Safely on the other side, the boat ascends Trent Lock, on the Erewash Canal.

Some boatmen assisted in the construction of bridges across the Thames, finding they could be paid high rates for carriage of building materials. One boatman used to carry punts and skiffs from Bossoms boatyard (just above Oxford) down to Henley Regatta every year. Bossoms, apart from being a traditional Thames yard, also built the narrow boat *Edith*.

The most hazardous job for a boatman was to work on the rivers, where floods could be very dangerous. In bad conditions the boatman had several alternatives: when going downstream, he either put the horse aboard and steered the boat with poles or the horse pulled the boat a little faster than the current to give the boat steerage. Coming upstream, the position was harder; either the boatman would hire horses from horse dealers who would also supply horse drivers (these were normally obtained at river/canal junctions, i.e. Oxford, Abingdon, Reading) or a group would join together and all the horses would pull one boat a short distance, and then they would go back and pull the next boat up, and so on. One particularly bad spot on the Thames was Abingdon Bridge, and here a winch was installed to help pull the boats upstream. Flash locks were a constant nuisance both in drought and flood and it has been known for up to a dozen horses to be used to get a boat through. The problems were not just confined to the Thames; Newbury Bridge, for example,

Fig. 180. A very long string of narrow boats being towed down the Severn to Gloucester.

on the River Kennet, had no towing path, and in times of flood a large wooden anchor was floated down from the lock and made fast to the craft wishing to go upstream and then used to pull it through. Many rivers were short of bridges and the horses were conveyed across the river in ferries which sometimes created problems and many horses had to be blindfold-ed, as they became restive when the boat rocked; others could only be coaxed to swim across. One of the longest crossings was that at Trent Junction.

An exciting trip was described to me by a retired Number One whose grandfather (also a Number One) bought a load of salt in bars from Stoke Prior (near Droitwich). He joined

Fig. 181. Arriving at the docks.

the river Severn which was in flood and had a very quick trip down the river with his pony aboard. He then went through the Thames & Severn Canal and had another quick trip down the flooded Thames. On arrival in London, he sold the salt at a high price because of the shortage caused by the floods.

The impression one gets is that Number Ones only owned one, or a pair of boats, but in fact many Number Ones owned several boats, paying somebody to run the other boats. People such as Ernest Thomas of Walsall or Emanuel Smith of Brentford started as Number Ones and grew into carrying companies in their own right.

Some boatmen had their adult children running the boats; when boys reached the age of eighteen they started on their own on one of their parents' boats. Services such as laundry might be performed by retired boat ladies who lived in canal-side cottages and if the children of the Number Ones used them, their parents would pay the bills when they passed.

It could be difficult for a Number One to start up in business unless his father gave him a boat. Usually, a boatman started by hiring a boat from a boatyard or a middle man such as a colliery agent, who would also expect that

Fig. 182. The destination, Gloucester, with goods being trans-shipped with Severn 'trows'. Note how these craft, with sturdier lines and wooden bollards, resemble river craft.

boatman to trade for him. When he had some money, the boatman could put down a deposit of, say, £25, and pay off the rest of the boat (which might cost £500; by 1953 prices were as high as £1500) by instalments. The instalments were paid on a trip basis rather than a calendar basis. Often the payments were of a flexible nature so if the boatman had been caught by ice he could postpone a payment. Usually his first boat was a second-hand one and he would gradually progress to a new one. When buying a new boat he had the alternative of either one built of top quality wood or cheap wood; the latter was usually purchased as a second boat to be run by a captain who would share the income on a 50:50 basis.

During the nineteen thirties Number Ones on the Grand Union suffered from the policy of the Grand Union Canal Carrying Company (G.U.C.C.) to undercut their rates, and also from the need to undertake more work after their conversion to diesel. They had no alternative but to sell out, and the majority turned to Samuel Barlow. As a result, that company gained some of the best boatmen on the canal and the boat-people stayed in the same craft but no longer owned their boats.

Likewise, the Oxford Canal Number Ones began to experience difficulties. At one time any boat arriving at Hawkesbury could obtain an instant cargo of coal but by the nineteen thirties they had to wait two to three weeks. As a result, the only boatmen to survive were those who had regular contracts.

The Number Ones not only traded in the south; on the Staffordshire and Worcestershire Canal they carried much coal from the Cannock pits down to Kidderminster and Stourport, serving the power stations, gas-works, and carpet works as well as navigating off the canal up to Wilden iron works. A group of Number Ones, nick-named 'The Gloucesters' carried hay up the Severn for the Cannock pit ponies and at the right time of the year the load was ballasted with apples, the backload, of course, being Cannock coal. The Worcester and Birmingham had horse-drawn Number Ones right into the nineteen fifties carrying coal to the Royal Worcester china works, and Charles Ballinger traded with some interesting motors which had their engine room astern of the living cabin.

Further north, Number Ones were the last

Fig. 183. A pair of Emanuel Smith's boats on the Grand Union.

to trade on the arms of the Shropshire Union Canal; then the famous bank breached and stranded the remaining craft, ending the trade completely.

After the Second World War various newcomers started up as Number Ones, which helped to maintain the tradition of canal carrying. When Willow Wren Canal Transport Services were formed in 1963 the boatmen were technically Number Ones, as they hired the boats and were self-employed. This, of course, gave them and the company a tax advantage.

Fig. 184. John Gould of Newbury, who carried regularly for T. Harrison Chaplin Limited from Newbury to Sunbury. His carrying came to an abrupt end with the closing of the Kennet and Avon Canal, but a court action and the legal right of navigation stopped the canal being closed by Act of Parliament in 1951.

Chapter Twelve
Powered Boats

Though the horse was to remain on the towpath for another century, already in the early nineteenth century mechanical methods of boat haulage were being attempted. In 1837 both the Bridgewater Canal and the Regent's Canal tried cable haulage; the London and North-Western Railway even used small steam locomotives running beside the Shropshire Union Canal to haul boats. On the Staffordshire and Worcestershire Canal electric overhead cables were tested. None of these experiments was successful, nor was the idea of long trains of tug-towed craft practical, since there were too many locks to be negotiated.

The invention of steam heralded the approach of the railways, but, as with the canal system, it took many years for the railway network to be completed. Meanwhile, the steam 'motor' boat began to oust the horse-boat – despite opposition from the older boatmen. However, steam motors were more suitable as tugs on long stretches of water than as narrow boats. Steam had little advantage over horses on the canals – speed was marginally better, but there was always the danger of bank erosion, and the engine (in the early Fellows Morton boats) took up 10 tons of space, which, in a 30-ton boat, was a high proportion. Where steam did have an advantage was in the fly traffic, where horses had to be frequently changed. But, due to the necessity of having a trained engineman to look after the engine, the steam narrow boat did not readily supplant the horse for family boating.

Experiments in steam propulsion date from 1797, but it was not until 1814 that the first boat propelled by steam was to carry passengers; not for another forty years did steam take its place in narrow boats. In 1852 a steam boat was tried out on the Kennet and Avon Canal, and in 1854 the Grand Junction Canal Company launched the first of its steam narrow boats, *Dart*. The fleet of steam boats resembled the motors of today, but had longer cabins and larger funnels. Steam tugs were mostly used on rivers and lock-free sections of canal, since they carried no cargo. At the end of the horse era most tunnels without a towpath would have had a tug. Generally tugs were shorter than motors.

Steamers had a disastrous history on the Grand Junction; it was a spark from one of these steamers which lit the gunpowder that blew up the 'blow up' bridge in Regent's Park. *The Hornet* gave the following account of the boatman in charge on December the 2nd, 1874:

'A peep at bargee character was afforded by the inquest in connection with the Regent's Park explosion. Bargee, in the witness-box, was not an individual of whom any community could feel proud. He was the incarnation of stolid ignorance. Ignorant men are always careless, and what carelessness can effect, the results of the terrible explosion which appalled the metropolis but too clearly proves. By all means let us have legislation to secure the safer conveyance of gunpowder and other explosive materials; but also let us have legislation for the purpose of making bargee less of a brute and more of a man.'

Again, it was the fumes from one of these unlucky steamers that suffocated a couple of men in Blisworth tunnel (after they had bumped into a couple of leggers). The net result was that the company installed extra air shafts in the tunnel. After these disasters, the Grand Junction Company sold out their steamers in the mid-eighteen seventies to Fellows Morton and Clayton, who built their fleet up to become the most respected in the country, offering an impeccable service.

The Grand Junction fleet was built up as a replacement for the Pickford traffic so, in effect, the Fellows Morton steamers served the same role as the Pickford boats. Like their earlier counterparts, the steamers from City Road basin carried mixed cargoes and ran to a regular time-table. The City Road boats travelled direct either to Birmingham or Leice-

Fig. 185. A pair of boats waiting to enter Islington tunnel in 1907. The plume of smoke can be seen from the tunnel tug. On the far left is a small Thames sailing barge with mast lowered ready to proceed to a canalside wharf.

ster and Nottingham whilst the Brentford Boats went as far as the trans-shipment sheds at Braunston. In the London area tugs were used mainly for towing sand and gravel from the West Drayton area to London and bringing rubbish out; in the Birmingham area steam tugs, and later diesel tugs, were used virtually up to the end of trading. One of their great assets was their self-propulsion through tunnels, saving leggers much hard work, and they were used on some quite short tunnels. The Trent and Mersey Company had one tug at Preston Brook with its own covered dry dock at Dutton, and another for its two short tunnels at Barnton and Saltisford but, surprisingly, although first considered in 1830, the tunnel tugs at Braunston and Blisworth did not start until the eighteen seventies, after the start of regular steam narrow-boat trading.

At that time the canal was narrow from Brentford to Birmingham. The so-called 'Brentford' boats were steamers which came up the Thames after loading directly from the ships in the London docks, and entered the Grand Union at Brentford. The boats going to Birmingham were nicknamed 'greasy 'ockers'. Various theories have been put forward for

this nickname but the best goes as follows: when the boats reached Itchington top lock a horse was produced from the stables by the pub which towed the butty between the single locks and the publican who looked after the horses was less than conscientious. One day a steamer and butty were approaching the lock with a young lad aboard who said to the

Fig. 186. The tug Buffalo after a repaint.

99

Fig. 187. A steam tug emerges from Blisworth tunnel. On the right can be seen the waiting horses.

captain, 'I'll go down and get a horse with greasy hocks,' and from that the expression caught on.

The steamers had a great reserve of power with the advantages of almost silent running. There were no direct controls between engine and steerer: the helmsman, due to the quietness of running, either gave verbal orders to the engineman or rang a small bell. The fuel burnt was coke and a loaded boat with butty in tow burned ten bags of fuel from Braunston to Bull's Bridge (Southall) – 87 miles. Between the boiler and engine a curtain was hung to prevent dust settling on the highly polished machinery when firing. A string hammock was slung athwartships in front of the boiler so

Fig. 188. The last of the Grand Union tunnel tugs, Hasty, *in dry dock.*

that the engineman could take a quick rest. A full head of steam would last from Itchington bottom lock to Braunston ($8\frac{1}{2}$ miles), so giving him the chance of a 'kip' for a couple of hours. Although this practice was unofficial, nobody minded as long as the engineman fulfilled his responsibilities in the economic use of fuel.

These steamers were so powerful they could easily push open a pair of lock gates against 12 inches of water, though if a skipper was caught in the act he was fined ten shillings (50p) on the spot; this practice was therefore especially common at night.

An idea of canal discipline can be gleaned from the following extract:

'From the Hertford County Records. "Liberty of St. Albans Division, Midsummer Sessions 1805."

'"Certificate of conviction of William Lisuione, the captain of two boats belonging to Messrs. Newell & Cotton for leaving in the night of February 20th last, on the Grand Junction Canal in the parish of Abbots Langley, the valves and cloughs of the locks nos. 65 & 68 open and running after the boats had passed, so as to misspend and waste the water thereof."

'"Certificate of the conviction of Thomas Beamish of Coventry, boatman, for suffering his boat or vessel to strike or run upon the lock 65 situate in the said parish of Abbots Langley." Similar certificate of the conviction of Richard Carwin who had the care of a flyboat belonging to Mr. Gothard, carrier, for damage to lock no. 69. "Certificate of the conviction of Edward Poulton, for not having previous to his bringing his boat or vessel into the lock 68. Shut the lower gates of such lock, and the sluices belongong thereto, before he had drawn the cloughs of the upper gates." Epiphany Sessions 1808, "James Atkins Committed to the House of Correction for drawing the valves of the power-gate of lock 79 belonging to the Grand Junction Canal, whereby water was misspent."'

The power of the steam engines was particularly useful when towing the boats up the flooded Trent and also towing several butties up the tidal Thames. A steamer coming up from the docks would drop off various horse-boats at riverside wharfs en route, first picking

Fig. 189. *A Fellows Morton and Clayton steamer on its scheduled trip passing through London. Note how the butty is only half laden.*

up, at Brentford, navigation lights, lifebuoys, anchors and a pair of sweeps (large oars). The boatmen did not like mooring against these wharves as their boats were flat-bottomed and the suction on the mud could stop them from floating as the tide rose. To overcome this thick ropes were run under the hull and as the tide rose they would be worked enabling water to flow under the hull and break the suction.

The narrow.boat *Holland*, loaded with barrels of treacle, once failed to respond to this treatment and had to remain submerged for a whole tide. Fortunately the *Buckby* was alongside so that the children, together with personal effects, were transferred from their cabin before it was inundated.

Steam narrow boats were continually in use; they were loaded and unloaded simultaneously and picked up another ready-loaded butty for the next journey, so reducing waiting time to a minimum. Butties often had different cargoes and destinations from the steamer towing them. A City Road steamer, for example, could collect a butty at Bull's Bridge which had come via Brentford. The steamer had a crew of four with two people on and two people off duty and they used to change over at set points rather than times. Those off duty would sleep in the cabin while the others were work-

ing. Coming up from City Road they would change at Greenford, Uxbridge, Cassiobury Park (just above Ironbridge lock), Boxmoor, Cowroast, Slapton, Stoke Hammond, Bradwell, Stoke Bruerne, Long Buckby, Long Itchington, Hatton, and Knowle, which now

Fig. 190. *The Saltley-built* Baroness. *The churning water gives a measure of its power. She had an iron hull and wooden bottom and was built in 1898; in 1915 she was converted to diesel and re-named* Briton.

Fig. 191. One of the official boats carrying guests at the opening of the Foxton Inclined Plane.

seem surprisingly close together. Discipline was harsh and the steerer would knock the side of the cabin with his foot when they approached the change-over point and there would be trouble if the crew did not hear it and appear in time. The butty boat was expected to supply two people at all times; generally it was run as a family boat. Where they had no children, husband and wife have been known to have no proper sleep for fifty-two hours – the time taken from London to Birmingham.

Fig. 192. The Dorothy being loaded with tubes at Stanton and Stavely's works.

The emphasis on speed was not in vain: often this was the decisive factor in the choice between rail or canal. Stewart and Lloyds (tube manufacturers) of Halesowen were, at the turn of the century, undecided whether to send a large export consignment by railway or canal to the London Docks, so they sent one trial load by canal and one by rail. The steamer went flat out down the Grand Union and arrived at Brentford just as the tide turned in its favour to speed them down to the docks; the pair of boats were unloaded before the trainload arrived, thus securing another contract for F.M.C.

On the Grand Union, Fellows Morton were not the only steam narrow-boat carriers: Chas. Nelson of Stockton had the *Jason* and *Jupiter* which used coal and produced volumes of black smoke. These craft were used exclusively for the carriage of cement and bore the trademark of a cockerel on cabin blocks. Taylor's boatyard in Chester built for a Northampton Carrier the *Sentinel*, powered by a Sentinel Steam engine from Shrewsbury. Steamers also travelled extensively to Leicester and Nottingham.

Steamers were beneficial on the Trent as they could combat the floods as well as improving communications at Erewash Junction.

For horse-boats this junction created considerable hazard. The horses were taken across the river by ferry while the boats were winched across from the far bank. On one occasion, when two boats were being pulled across, the rope parted; the leading craft ran on to the head of the island, now the Trent Valley sailing club headquarters, while the second boat was swept down the weir stream, colliding, broadside on, with a railway bridge upstream of the completely unprotected weir. This boat was carrying sugar which dissolved and was immediately washed away as a result of the alarming angle at which the boat came to rest.

Fellows Morton and Clayton amongst others campaigned for the introduction of the 'inclined plane' at Foxton, where previously the levels of the Grand Union and the Leicester Section were equalized by a staircase of locks. The principle of the inclined plane was a mechanical lift, which, holding the narrow boats, ran down an incline on rails. Unfortunately the machinery was so costly to run that it

Fig. 193. The coal wharf at Cromford.

was abandoned a few years after it was opened in 1900.

The steamers also traded to Derby and, as in the other runs, butties were picked up which had loaded at other wharves. Although today it is a short cul-de-sac, the Erewash and its connections generated much trade. Stanton and Stavely's works were situated on the adjoining Nutbrook Canal and, amongst other things, they exported via the Erewash all the steelwork for the 'Sydney Harbour' type pipe bridge below Derwent Mouth lock. The adjoining Cromford Canal terminated at Arkwright's own mill, the birthplace of the industrial revolution. Further down, the canal was served by lead mines and quarries and Ironville, an example of a mid-nineteenth century company village, whose products included the ironwork supporting the roof of St Pancras Station, was built on its banks. The bottom end of the Cromford Canal provided waterborne coal until the early 'fifties. The Derbyshire and Nottinghamshire coalfields competed successfully for London orders, and provided coal to Croxley right up to 1943. Amongst other outlets were Leicester and Loughborough power stations. Ellis and Everard, the well-known East Midland builder's merchant

then also coal merchants, had a pair, *Evelyn* and *Hilda*, which carried to various wharves as well as supplying the Grand Junction Tunnel tugs.

The steam boats were the last of a line of all-male crews following the traditions of the fly-boats. The captain was paid so much a trip and it was up to him to pay the crew. By all accounts their predominant diet was salted

Fig. 194. Thornycroft's gas suction engine boat Duchess.

Figs 195 & 196. Edward Tailby's motor boat Progress *on the Worcester and Birmingham Canal; the bows of the boats are typical of craft using that canal.*

beef and there was little time for the everyday tasks such as shopping and washing. It was customary for the crew to wear white cord trousers and white overalls.

It was inevitable that, in time, an alternative to steam would be sought. The first experiment was with the *Vulcan* in 1911, a steamer to which a suction gas engine built by Crossleys of Manchester was fitted; Thornycroft fitted out the ex-steamer *Duchess* in

1906, with their own 30 h.p. gas motor which consumed 30lb of anthracite per hour when loaded and towing a laden butty. Other experiments included fitting a 20 h.p. high-speed steam engine to the narrow boat *Thistle* in 1909. The Shropshire Union Company tried crude petrol-driven drive units on their *Waterlily* and another horse-boat. The *Progress* was designed and built by Edward Tailby of Birmingham. Running on paraffin, it carried out

Fig. 197. Cadbury Brothers were one of the first carriers to use diesel engines. This early photograph shows the resplendent boats.

Figs 198 & 199. Soon Cadburys changed their lettering to a more modern style and later employed the Severn and Canal Carrying Company for transport of goods to and from Gloucester.

trials on the Worcester and Birmingham Canal in 1907 before an epic voyage to London.

The real takeover from horse power was the diesel engine, of which the semi-diesel was the prototype. Fellows Morton's first was the *Linda*, which went into service in 1912. At the same time the *Lynx* was being built as a steam engine, but the success of the diesel was such that the design was altered to accommodate a diesel engine. It soon became apparent that the Bolinders (the single cylinder semi-diesel engines) were more satisfactory than the steamers – they took up far less cargo space – and soon the steamers were converted to diesel, or sold off. By 1927 the last of the Fellows Morton steamers had stopped running. By then the Bolinder was commonplace throughout the system, but the Grand Union fleet, which was begun in 1931, used various engines, including Petter, National and Russell Newbury.

The problem with a Bolinder was that it had to be heated with a blow-lamp before it would start. It produced a very distinctive noise, and being single-cylinder it was low revving. It had no reverse gear as such; in practice, the engine was backfired to put the boat astern. This was done by slowing the engine right down and pulling a lever which injected fuel at the right moment to cause it to backfire. The whole engine would stop dead in its tracks and would therefore begin to move in the opposite direction.

One Number One had his horse-boat converted at Bushell Brothers. When he collected the boat, the Bolinder representative gave him a quick explanation on how to use the engine and he set forth up the Wendover Arm at full throttle. When he approached the junction, he thought that all he had to do was pull a lever – he was mistaken, as he realized to his cost when the boat charged straight across the Main line and into the opposite bank! His blaspheming could be heard across the fields. With great reluctance he towed his boat back by hand, where it had to stay for another week while it was repaired. From then on he never forgot to cut the revs right down before pulling the magic lever.

One big advantage of the Bolinders was their durability, and many outlived their hulls and were transferred to other boats. In the last few years of their narrow boat fleet, British Waterways carried out an extensive refitting programme using Petter air-cooled diesels, which unfortunately did not give very good service.

Fig. 200. British Waterways fitting a new motor to a motor boat at Bull's Bridge.

Chapter Thirteen
1850-1918

As we saw in Chapter One, the coming of the railways stopped further canal-building and eroded canal traffic. In most cases, canal companies collapsed at the prospect of the competition from railways, but one notable exception was the Shropshire Union. In 1846 the Shropshire Union Railways and Canal Company was formed as an amalgamation of the Birmingham and Liverpool Canal, Ellesmere and Chester Canal, the Montgomeryshire Canal, the Shrewsbury and Newport and other branches. With the canal system stretching into Great Western Railway territory, these canals were used as an extension to the railway. One unusual aspect of the system was that the canal company had its own fleet which operated a monopoly. At its peak in 1889, the company had three hundred and ninety five narrow boats. There had been a recession in the eighteen sixties when the American Civil War slowed down the Birmingham traffic destined to be exported via Liverpool. Much of the prosperity of the canal was based upon early iron works in the Coalbrookdale area and Trevor. As the industrial revolution advanced, the iron from these areas, along with coal from Chirk, became redundant, and trade dwindled to agriculture and through traffic. The Shropshire Canal was used in conjunction with railways, interchange depots being in the Birmingham area. In 1921, the company sold its fleet of two hundred and two craft and opened the canal to general traders. It was taken over by the L.M.S. in 1922. Many of the craft were bought by people already using the canal, such as Peates of Maesbury Mill, Oswestry, and Arthur Sumner of Wrenbury.

Fig. 201. Boats held up by fallen trees, February 1910.

Fig. 202. Sephsons sunken narrow boat at Great Linford, August 1912.

Fig. 203. The Shropshire Union warehouse at Ellesmere, Salop.

Fig. 204. The Shropshire Union Railway and Canal Company's depot at Ellesmere Port.

The Shropshire Union Railway and Canal Company had an interchange depot at Barbridge. Here vessels capable of crossing the Mersey could travel up the wide locks from Chester and trans-ship to the narrow boats, it being a very convenient point as it was also close to Hurleston Junction. The S.U. company regularly traded as far afield as Warwick conveying grain from Ellesmere Port. The Shropshire Union Company tried experimental canal towage in 1888 on the Middlewich Branch. A small Crewe locomotive was run on an 18-inch gauge track on the towpath. Although the experiment proved successful, a scheme for laying track over any length was never adopted, probably because of the prohibitive cost.

The other big carrier of this period was Fellows Morton and Clayton. In a similar way to the S.U.R. & C. Co. they had a large interchange depot at Preston Brook. Here, Mersey flats would change cargoes with narrow boats. Much tinned food was placed in warehouses and then transported to Nottingham and Birmingham while manufactured goods were brought to the warehouses to await shipment. One of their specialities was cooking pots, and to this day one of the warehouses is referred to as 'the pot shed'. Fellows Morton had a gentleman's agreement with the Manchester Ship Canal concerning renting warehouses. The system worked well and not until nationalization was it realized that there was nothing in writing.

Despite their size, F.M. & C. paid as much attention to small contracts as large and would often have boats specially built for a given cargo. They also leased boats which were painted up in the colours of the companies concerned, although this was not very common. Fellows Morton were one of the few national carriers in the south; they kept pace with technology by introducing steamers, used

Fig. 205. An F.M.C. butty with a load of tinned goods for Nottingham.

Fig. 206. Fellows Morton & Clayton boats loading at Runcorn. The canal is now filled in.

their influence on canal companies to improve their canals and instigated the building of the Foxton Inclined plane (see previous chapter). They also pressed for better concessions on through rates especially where a given cargo travelled through various canal companies' territory. The improvements that F.M.C. strived for came between the wars but unfortunately with them came a large new fleet which competed fiercely with Fellows Morton.

Fig. 207. Fellows Morton and Clayton had a fleet of steam lorries and horse-carts to convey goods from the canal to factories.

Chapter Fourteen
Between the Wars

In the north life on the canals in the 'thirties did not change much, but in the south great changes came about. Whilst the Shropshire Union boats after World War I were still horse-drawn, in the south during the 'twenties diesel narrow boats were introduced by several companies. Though canals were losing trade, new projects of expansion were still launched, the greatest of which was the modernization of the Grand Union network. On January 1st, 1929, the Grand Union Canal Company came into being, forming an amalgamation of five companies: the Regent's Canal Company, the Grand Junction Canal, the Birmingham and Warwick, the Warwick and the Napton. Birmingham was linked with the Thames at Limehouse and Brentford and the Regent's Canal Dock, and then, three years later, the remainder of the Leicester Line to Langley Mills was also included.

The new company set about improving the canal routes, mainly widening the Napton to Birmingham section from 7 feet to 14 feet, and doing much needed maintenance on the rest of the system. They realized that new trade was not going to come to the canal system unless they set about trying to attract it, and decided that the best method of doing so was to set up their own carrying company. The first step was that the Grand Union Company bought Associated Canal Carriers of Northampton in 1929. This company, along with one pair of boats, the *George* and *Mary*, which were bought by the Grand Union Company and delivered a month after the merger, formed the basis of their carrying fleet. Associated Canal Carriers started to expand. They bought a series of boats from various boatyards, usually a pair from each, and also some second-hand boats. Then in 1934 A.C.C. launched an expansion programme, the object of which was to increase the fleet to a hundred pairs. At this point the name was changed to the Grand Union Canal Carrying Company. During 1934, some prototype boats were built, but from 1935 onwards the boats all came from Walkers

of Rickmansworth, Harland and Wolfe of Woolwich or Yarwoods at Northwich, and they were all 'town' or 'star' class boats, wooden or steel.

Soon after this the Grand Union Canal Carrying Company established its depot at Bull's Bridge where a lay-by was constructed for boats to await orders to load either at Brentford or Regent's Canal Dock; the depot also had dry docks, wet docks and slips, offices and all the general trades associated with repairing canal craft. By the end of 1938, the Grand Union Canal Carrying Company fleet had increased to a total of three hundred and seventy-three boats which made it almost as large as the Shropshire Union Canal Carrying Company at its peak. With this new modern fleet traffic soon increased on the canal and whenever possible the Grand Union Company obtained new traffic for the canal rather than take it from other carriers, although unfortunately they did take the Croxley traffic away

Fig. 208. Work on widening the canal at Braunston. The narrow boat in the centre of the picture is in the old seven-foot wide section.

Fig. 209. British Waterways boats moored at Bull's Bridge depot, Southall.

Fig. 210. Boats loading just downstream of Brentford town lock. A large pair of royalty class can be seen on the right and a girl class F.M.C. butty on the left.

Fig. 211. The Grand Union Canal Carrying Company wide boat Progress *being built at Tring.*

from the Number Ones. The expansion programme created certain problems, one being to find enough crews to man the new boats, the second being that although the carrying company had made a profit, this profit was not large enough to cover the return on investment, as the boats had been financed by an investment company at the rate of 6%. The biggest problem was that they had built too many boats. Because of the unavailability of boatmen, the company rarely worked more than a hundred pairs at any one time; had the company only built half the number of new boats they could have found enough crews to man them, whereas, having such a large fleet, this became impossible. The position was further aggravated during the Second World War when many crewmen joined up, and, during those difficult times, the company was forced to use women recruits. One of the best achievements of this great fleet was that it helped to continue canal carrying into the nineteen sixties. By then many of the existing boats were unfit for commercial use.

The widening of the G.U. to Birmingham not only helped the Grand Union fleet, it also helped trade in general and it soon made the horse obsolete from London to Birmingham. During the steamer days Fellows Morton had often used horses to tow the butties and the steamer had gone singly up this section, because of the number of locks. The other advantage was on the Leicester line: a journey from the Trent to Watford junction previously meant travelling through different canal carrying companies' territories with a multitude of tolls, some of which were blatantly exorbitant. This way, one toll for the journey could be agreed.

During the nineteen thirties, canal carrying was regarded as a worthwhile supplement to road transport, the biggest competitor still being rail. It became customary for the canals to supply raw materials in bulk to London and other towns and from there the goods were transported by road to their destination. During this period there was a large number of wharfs on the canal in London, where goods would be transferred into small lorries for dispersal across the metropolis, and canal traffic could still be very competitive with railways when goods were trans-shipped on indirect lines; often goods stayed many days in railway sidings, making canal deliveries faster. The Grand Union Company, with its large resources, opened up several other companies, the main ones being the Grand Union Shipping Ltd, and the Grand Union Stevedore and Wharfage Company Ltd, whose job was to run ships to serve Regent's Canal Dock and hence the canal trade. They ran weekly services to Antwerp and Rotterdam. These ships, in fact, brought completely new trade to the canal which represented over twenty per cent of the total carried. The other improvement made by the Grand Union was the expansion of canal depots: Samson Road and Tyseley, Brentford, Northampton and Leicester were all enlarged and improved. Here goods could be delivered and stored and, as previously mentioned, in those days of small-volumed lorries it was often very convenient for customers in these areas. Often a small producer would not have room to store a large amount of material on his own premises but a shipload could quite easily be stored at these depots. These services expanded the canal transport system as a whole.

The coming of the Second World War altered the nature of canal carrying as it was run under government control and, of course, very soon after the end of the war, it was nationalized. In October 1932 the Severn and Canal Carrying Company introduced a new type of narrow boat – their first diesel. She was built at their boatyard at Stourport, and designed by C.B. Hinman. Like other craft belonging to the company, the hull was similar to the Runcorn boats in that it had little shape and wooden bollards. The motor was used both on the river and the Staffordshire and Worcester Canal. This canal, apart from being one of the oldest in the country, continued to make a profit right up to nationalization. Horse traffic survived on it until the 'fifties, mostly being day boats. The boats would load at the Cannock pits and were brought down the Hatherton Branch. One set

Fig. 212. The Duke of Kent opening the Hatton flight of locks aboard Progress.

of boatmen would take the boats down to Stewpony and return with the empty craft, which had been left there the night before, while another set of men took them on to Stourport power station and back.

Fig. 213. Barrels of spice being loaded directly into a narrow boat for shipment for H.P. sauce, Birmingham.

Chapter Fifteen
From World War II to the Present Day

In 1948 the canals, along with most of the canal carriers, were nationalized. The greatest part of the fleet was contributed by Fellows. Morton and Clayton and the Grand Union Canal Carrying Company. However, independent canal carriers still operated. At this time Fellows Morton and Clayton were still having new hulls built and the *Mendip* and *Malvern* were not commissioned until after nationalization. It was during the preceding year that Fellows Morton and Clayton made their first loss. Boatmen argue that this was due to a backlog of bad maintenance of boats. The early years of nationalization had little effect on the boatmen except perhaps that the standards of maintenance went up; much effort was put into painting the boats. Whereas the canal carrying companies would have removed an area of rot, and put in some stopping, making the job do for another twelve months, British Waterways would replace the whole thing with new wood.

British Waterways also improved the conditions of the boatmen. They gained in financial security: for the first time they had paid holidays and a minimum wage when they were tied up. By the end of nationalization the boatmen could claim quite a few extras. For example, in the north-west, when travelling with a butty, extra was paid at flights of narrow locks to compensate for the inconvenience in the double-locking. This was paid for Audlem, Adderley, and Tyrely on the Shropshire Union, the Wolverhampton flight, and the Trent and Mersey from Harecastle to Middlewich. Extra was also paid if the boats had to go a longer way round because of stoppages; for cleaning out boats after a dirty cargo; for travelling fly; the return of empty bags; part cargo; split cargoes; Sunday working in Manchester docks; standing by all night to receive cargo from Manchester docks only; navigating the River Trent without a pilot, and for time wasted whilst craft were in dock.

The basic rate was still calculated as a basic rate per ton for every route used. Hence the extra for part loads, and a flat rate for travelling empty. Near the end of nationalization (1962) in the north-west, the guaranteed weekly wage was in excess of £10 for a pair of boats and, considering that there were no rent, rates, or fuel bills to pay, it represented a reasonable wage. Some boatmen felt this had a negative effect; they reckoned that others took advantage and, when in a lazy mood, it could pay them to have an engine breakdown.

Later, British Waterways ran into heavy financial problems, and, to try and offset this, capital was used to build new boats to save on maintenance. In theory the idea was good: fibreglass hatch covers saved large expense on renewing top and sidecloths which had a relatively short life, while an all-welded cabin saved much woodwork, and paint keyed better to steel so the boats needed less frequent repainting. But the new boats were criticized; they tended to be ugly in comparison to their predecessors, and, worse, their handling quali-

Fig. 214. A large Rickie butty boat on the slips at Bull's Bridge having her planks re-caulked.

ties were poor. Some received major altera-
tions to shape, while others were never used.
This produced bad morale within the boat-
people as they were forced to use boats they
didn't like, and damaged their relationship
with their employers.

In the long run, the admiral class motors
and two Yarwood butties played an invaluable
part in keeping narrow boat transport going
into the 'seventies. Further economies were
made by using transfers (for roses and castles)
and simplifying the colour scheme. Occasional
dissatisfaction was felt by the boatmen that
their lives were in the hands of a bureaucratic
machine which did not know much about
canals and which was out of sympathy with
much of the boat-people's way of life. Further
aggravation was caused by British Waterways'
insistence on equipment being signed for; a
practice that embarrassed the illiterate boatman.

Winter 1962-3 was the coldest for many
decades, and canal traffic was at a standstill
for months; but, though the times seemed
gloomy, in fact they produced a new lease of
life for the canals. The toll system – the
system of paying a fixed fee per ton per mile to
the canal company, which varied according to
the merchandise – was abolished. Instead an
annual licensing system was introduced, with
a fee of £25 a year, which entitled one to use all
canals without further tolls. British Waterways denationalized its carrying side (except
for four pairs) and it was absorbed into Willow
Wren who, in turn, changed their name to
Willow Wren Canal Transport Services. Willow Wren hired the boats from British Waterways and in turn hired the boats to the
boatmen and provided them with work. The
boatmen had to provide all necessary ropes
and diesel fuel, and were responsible for maintenance. One liability taken away from the
company was standing money. If the boats
had to wait for a cargo, ice, floods or stoppages,
the boatmen could collect unemployment benefit, thus saving the company quite a large
annual bill.

In 1948 a large number of boats and private
carriers were still using the canal system. It is
interesting to recall how British Waterways
traded up and down the Runcorn locks, which
are now filled in, as well as carrying rock salt
from Seddons to Macclesfield. Coal was car-

*Fig. 215. Grain being loaded into narrow
boats at Brentford for Wellingborough.*

ried to Worcester porcelain works for Worcester china from Cannock by private enterprise
with a reverse traffic of cocoa to Cadbury's at
Bournville. One well-known trip was Charlie
Atkins' thirteen-year stint of carrying choco-
late chips between Knighton and Bournville –
Cadbury's factory on the Shropshire Union –
twice a week. Harvey Taylor of Aylesbury
carried mainly to and from Aylesbury as well
as taking sand from Leighton Buzzard as far
as Birmingham, for glass-making, while in
earlier years, grain was picked up at bridge
holes as was milk. Other grain was loaded at
Leighton Buzzard from the towpath under a
little hump bridge just on the sharp bend
below the main road bridge. In the end one
pair with boatmen was taken over by Barlows.
Faulkeners of Leighton Buzzard wilted, while
Wyvern shipping of Leighton Buzzard
gradually changed from cargo-carrying to
pleasure boating. In the early days, their fleet
was based on ice-breakers, tugs and narrow
boats.

One reason for the decline was that both
staff and boats were old; if a big contract was
lost, the managers felt it was time to retire.
The boats were in poor condition and capital
was not available to build new boats. In the
case of Thos. Clayton at Oldbury, their boatyard was acquired to build a motorway in
1966, and with an old fleet of wooden boats
which were on their last legs, and with low
profit margins, the company could not justify
more expenditure.

Similar reasons applied to Mersey Weaver
and the old Anderton Company. The Ovaltine

Fig. 216. Boats waiting to unload at Welling-borough.

boats, along with S.E. Barlow of Tamworth, carried coal to their works, but wooden boats and a change to oil stopped the fleet. The pattern seemed to be that if one company failed, for example, to keep to schedules, the traffic would be transferred to road rather than another canal carrier. Sometimes traffic would be lost when canalside factories or canalside collieries closed. Recently, the building of the Tilbury grain terminal in 1969, which made the overland journey through London easier, not only stopped the largest remaining contract (taking grain to Welling-borough) but also the last wooden barges trading on the Thames and the River Wey.

As traffic diminished, many contracts had to be turned down because of the small number of boats available. If a shipload, for example, came in once a month, it would be impossible

Fig. 217. Boats unloading at Wellingborough.

to have enough boats to carry the large tonnage when it arrived, and then the boats would be idle for the following three weeks. In the old days one company could call on the resources of many other companies and could, say, carry a shipload of timber one week, ingots another, then grain, spices, tea, and back to timber again. There was also a constant traffic on most canals, which meant the channel would be kept clear and any other carrier knew that he could get a loaded pair of boats along without going aground. In recent times, new traffic had to be restricted to a small number of canals in order to keep the channel free. The more silted up the canal became, the smaller the loads boats could carry, which made them less economic.

So a controversy exists about the effects of nationalization: on one side, British Waterways achieved a great deal. Canals like the main line of the Shropshire Union were much improved after nationalization. Favourable annual licensing was granted, along with small rental for boats, and there was a limit to how much public money could be spent on subsidizing a carrying fleet. Even when canal carriers finished trading, the boatmen were allowed to stay on in British Waterways rented boats. However, on little-used sections of canal, British Waterways did not feel they could justify spending money dredging a particular section of canal for one carrier who had just gained a small contract, considering he might only keep it for a few months. In one case, a dredger escorted the first pair so that any large obstruction in bridges, etc., could be cleared.

On the other hand British Waterways were largely responsible for the decline of waterway traffic because they left annual licensing too late and they should have realized that it paid to have narrow boats on the canal because they kept the channel clear. The 'economy' of cutting out gate paddles on lock gates slowed the boats down. One of the biggest criticisms was that there was no guarantee of the length of time that annual licensing would stay and the scheme was only renewed yearly. It was also argued that if private enterprise could continue trading profitably, British Waterways could have spent the money better on other schemes instead of on building better narrow boats and improving the standard of maintenance.

Fig. 218. One of the early waterways campaigns was to secure the removal of the girders from under this bridge spanning the Kennet and Avon Canal in Reading. The boats would float up to the bridge; the water level was dropped, the boats then went through and waited until the water had risen enough for them to proceed.

One big change since the war has been the switch of competition from railways to roads; the large lorries buzzing down the M1 past Buckby locks at seventy while the boatman waited for the lock to fill must surely have made him feel his life on the boats could not go on for ever. It is surprising how so many boatmen stayed on to the very end; by the mid-sixties wages had dropped and it can only have been the way of life which kept them on: a habit difficult to break and the inability to settle on the land. Michael Street, who ran Blue Line Canal Carriers, who had the last three pairs regularly trading between the Midlands and London, says: 'One by one, over the ensuing years, the small firms faded and died. The dock yards closed, the boatmen and their families left the cabins for the last time and took dull, highly paid 40-hour week jobs, turning up now and again at the regular mooring places in their third-hand Consuls, Zodiacs and Crestas, to chat with those who still remained afloat, earning an average wage of £3 10s. 0d. per head for a 10-hour day, winter and summer. And who envied who was never really clear, for if you and your parents before you (and theirs before them) were born in a narrow-boat cabin and knew no other life, the hold of habit is powerful and dies hard. And it was this that ensured that the narrow boat survived so long; not, alas, its intrinsic superiority over road and rail, but the simple, brutal fact that because they knew no better, canal boatmen, their wives and children worked eighteenth-century hours, for nineteenth-

Fig. 219. With the possibility of being held up by ice, this pair of boats is outflanked by the hundred-mile-an-hour freightliner.

century pay, until three-quarters of the way through the twentieth century. Years ago, it was nothing less than naked exploitation. British Waterways tried to meet it by paying better wages; that increased charges to the customer and the marginal cost advantage of the boat was lost, and so was the trade, until in the end they reached the inescapable conclusion that they couldn't go on.'

British Waterways Board, when it replaced the Waterways Commission in 1962, began a detailed study of the inland waterways, the results of which were presented to the Government in the *Facts About Waterways* in 1965. The conclusions were that only the major waterways were commercially viable, the

Fig. 220. The last export consignment: salt being unloaded at Weston Point Docks in 1970. By using the ship's derricks, dock charges were reduced.

115

Fig. 221. *Returning empty up the Weaver aboard the* Mountbatten *with destination Preston Brook, a working day away. Now that the motorway in the background is finished, it takes a juggernaut less than five minutes.*

others were not. However, the cost of even abandoning all these canals was estimated to be approximately £600,000 p.a., and for another £340,000 p.a. the Board believed it could maintain the canals for the benefit of pleasure craft. This recommendation was finally accepted in 1967, and our canal system has received a much-needed subsidy to provide

Fig. 222. *The large Northwich* Nutfield *and the Nurser butty* Lucy *head south with one of the last regular consignments of coal from the Midlands to London.*

leisure facilities.

Fortunately the traditions of canal carriage are kept alive by enthusiasts. During the summer several unconverted narrow boats convey parties of young people on camping trips and during the winter the same boats sometimes take cargoes of coal to more populated areas where they endeavour to sell it for domestic use.

The last regular surviving narrow boat traffic is the carriage of lime juice from Brentford to Messrs. Roses at Boxmoor. This was continued by three pairs of British Waterways board craft until 1972 and has now been taken over by various small concerns including Messrs. Three Fellows Canal Carrying.

In Birmingham there is still one carrier left – the last of the horse-drawn carriers – Mr 'Caggy' Stevens, who carries refuse in his day boats, which are either towed by his horse or by the tug *Caggy*. In various parts of the country there are horse-drawn pleasure boats, many of which are converted commercial craft. Today they operate at Chester, Berkhamsted, Newbury, Llangollen and Norbury Junction.

On the Trent and Mersey Canal (Caldon Branch), two specially built narrow boats, the *Milton Maid* and the *Milton Queen*, carry china for **Johnson** Brothers at Hanley. Josiah Wedgewood, the great eighteenth-century potter, was one of the promoters of the Trent and Mersey and now, to complete the two-hundred-year cycle, Johnson Brothers are part of the Wedgewood Group.

Several museums now have restored narrow boats: the excellent British Waterways Museum at Stoke Bruerne on the Grand Union near Towcester, Northants; the Cheddleton Flint Mill Industrial Heritage Trust; and the North-West Museum of Inland Navigation, which has been established at Ellesmere Port.

In October 1977 the Black Country Museum opened alongside the Dudley Canal at Tipton. A short arm runs into the site where a traditional boatyard is being constructed; the dock is to be a working exhibit and will appear as it might have done at the turn of the century. The museum at present has four working boats. The idea is to demonstrate boatbuilding skills while restoring and maintaining these craft.

Fig. 223. The inevitable end: disused day boats in a disused canal. Even the optimists never believed that canals would ever become popular again.

Bibliography

Chaplin, Tom, *A Short History of the Narrow Boat* (Hugh McKnight, 1974).

Faulkner, Alan H., *The George and Mary* (Robert Wilson, 1973). *F.M. & C.* (Robert Wilson, 1973).

Jones, Barbara, *The Rose and Castle: The Unsophisticated Arts* (Architectural Press, 1951).

Lansdell, Avril, *Clothes of the Cut*, (B.W.B., 1976).

Lewery, A.J., *Narrow Boat Painting* (David & Charles, 1974).

McKnight, Hugh, *Vessels of the Waterways of England and Holland: The Decorative Art of the Mariner* (Cassell, 1966).

Rolt, L.T.C., *Narrow Boat* (Eyre & Spottiswode, 1944).

Smith, Emma, *Maiden's Trip* (Putnam, 1948).

Smith, George, *Our Canal Population 1870* (reprinted E.P., 1974).

Wilkinson, Tim, *Hold on a Minute* (Allen & Unwin, 1965).

Wilson, Robert J., *The Number Ones* (Robert Wilson, 1972). *Boatyards and Boatbuilding* (Robert Wilson, 1974). *Knobsticks* (Robert Wilson, 1975). *Life Afloat* (Robert Wilson, 1976). *Roses and Castles* (Robert Wilson, 1976).

Index